40 women share inspiring stories
compass, focus on positive habits, and lead life with purpose.

THE DECONSTRUCTING G.R.I.T. COLLECTION

COMPILED BY
JENNIFER BARDOT

INTENTION - Deconstructing G.R.I.T. Collection
40 women share inspiring stories of how they listen to their own internal compass, focus on positive habits, and lead life with purpose.
MDC Press

Published by **MDC Press**, St. Louis, MO
Copyright ©2023
All rights reserved.

All contributing authors to this anthology have submitted their chapters to an editing process, and have accepted the recommendations of the editors at their own discretion. All authors have approved their chapters prior to publication.

Cover, Interior Design, and Project Management:
  Davis Creative Publishing, DavisCreativePublishing.com
Writing Coach and Editor: Maria Rodgers O'Rourke

Compilation by Jennifer Bardot

Names: Bardot, Jennifer, compiler.
Title: Intention : the deconstructing G.R.I.T. collection / compiled by Jennifer Bardot.
Other titles: Intention GRIT
Description: St. Louis, MO : MDC Press, [2023]
Identifiers: ISBN: 978 1 7371848 6 7 (paperback) | 978 1 7371848 7 4 (ebook) |
  LCCN: 2023909245
Subjects: LCSH: Intention Literary collections. | Intention Anecdotes. | Self actualization (Psychology) in women Literary collections. | Self actualization (Psychology) in w omen Anecdotes. | Will Literary collections. | Will Anecdotes. | Determination (Personality Literary collections. | Determination (Personality trait) Anecdotes. | LCGFT: Anecdotes.
Classification: LCC: BF611 .I58 2023 | DDC: 153.8 dc23

This book is dedicated to
my children, my nieces, and nephews.
My wish for each of you is that you
become the captain of your life.

Table of Contents

Jennifer Bardot | Introduction 1

Jennifer Bardot | Own YOUR Future 3

Dr. Karen Hall | Educating for Change 9

Roberta Moore | The Call That Changed My Life 15

Taryn Pulliam | A Path of My Own 21

Debi Corrie | Taking Intentional Risks 27

Angela Pinon | Intention – Education – Celebration 33

Kimberly Lebbing | Embracing the Storms 39

Rachel Rubin Wilkins | G.O.A.L. Go Out And Live! 45

Natalie Goeckeler | I Pfeiffered It! 52

Kristene Rosser | KMA, I'm Doing It Anyway 58

Jennifer Church | Dream Big 64

Danielle Tabers | My Superhero Mindset 70

Dr. Tiffany E. Slater | Intentionally Faithful 76

Kim Robertson | Playing Through the Sand Traps 81

Amanda Bohnert | Seeking to Engage, Elevate & Lead 87

Becki Feldmann | Stop Wishing, Start Doing 94

Sally Drake | Iron Intention 100

Nikki MacDonald | A Woman's Touch 106

Shalia Ford | I Choose Me 112

Karen Englert | Gifts of Desperation and Grace 118

Suzy Barbosa-McBride | From Multicolored Flower to Me 124

Luciana Sabatino Cross | The Silver Lining 130

Monique Block Bynum | Cleared for Takeoff 136

Marcy Bursac | Reveal Your Heart's Intention 141

Sabrina Westfall | Intention Is My GPS 148

Alison Niermann | Release and Rise Up 154

Ly Syin Lobster | Sobriety, Faith, and Intention 160

Maureen Hergenroether | Check Your Impact 166

Kimberly Rayford | Staying on the Path 172

Stephanie Enger-Moreland | Finding My Way to Helping Others . 178

Lori Drury | Cultivating Intentional Relationships 184

Lusnail Haberberger | Bringing *Familia* to Corporate America . . . 190

Dr. Jade D. James-Halbert | Divine Intention 196

Tina Asher | Own Your Day 202

Dr. Roslyn Grant | A Legacy of Intention 208

Jessica Lopez-Liggett | Shaping Your Destiny,
        Defying Circumstances 214

Melanie Siebert | Create Your Own Destiny 220

Vidya Thandra Satyanarayana | Rise and Shine 226

Maura Caldwell-Thompson | Letting Go of Holding On 232

Gina Sweet | Intentional Love 238

Jennifer Bardot

Introduction

Intentions are maps we use to chart our journeys. They guide us toward calm waters, blue skies, and steady winds. They are there when we are being tossed in a churning sea or stuck in the doldrums. They build our resilience by helping us focus on the ebb and flow of threatening events and the achievement of success. As leaders, we are called upon to captain the ship and be prepared to change course when challenges arise, which they always will. Each intention is a goal, each goal is a vision that fuels our reality. Our thoughts, values, beliefs, and behaviors are our sailboats. Without intention, we are adrift, living in uncertainty. The stories in this book reflect the courage, vision, and achievements of women bravely traveling on their journeys, learning from mistakes, and growing beyond their frailties—all with intention.

Jennifer Bardot

Own YOUR Future

"Ponder and deliberate before you make a move." —Sun Tzu

It hit me in 2017 while sitting in my parents' basement on maternity leave with my third child: What had I achieved since my master's degree? I had deprioritized myself and my career while building my family. My family had always come before anything else, and I had three beautiful children. But what was my purpose beyond being "Mom"? The past eight years I had worked full time, juggled motherhood, but I hadn't pushed myself since graduate school. In 2009, at twenty-six years of age, I completed two master's degrees, made the Dean's List, worked full time, had two internships, held a graduate assistantship, and graduated with only $15,000 in student loans.

Those three years I had clarity and I hit my goal. "A goal is a dream with a deadline," said Napoleon Hill. What I achieved in graduate school prior to having children provided me proof that I was capable of striving for more, but the self-doubt persisted. Sleepless with a newborn and juggling my two children who needed additional requirements for IEP (Independent Educational Plans) speech services with my oldest also dealing with ongoing health issues made it seem impossible to focus on my career. Now a mother of three and working in a nonprofit as a financial aid coordinator, I studied the wealth gap. These alarming deficits of finances for women gave me the motivation to personally advance the economic ladder. Seven years had now passed, and at thirty-three it was time to focus on my career aspirations and "have it all": a family, a career, and the ability to support the community. Sitting in my parents' basement, I set this intention.

I had hit rock bottom. My oldest child kept getting sick. For example, for six days in kindergarten he carried a 105.6 fever. My gut told me something was seriously wrong when my three-month-old wasn't getting sick. I was drowning in medical debt, sadness, feeling hopeless, and my anxiety was soaring. My employer was irritated as I had to work remotely to take care of my child, and I was emotionally exhausted. I temporarily moved in with my parents because I thought that my home was causing this sickness, but the sickness continued at my parents'. I was depleted. He was constantly getting strep throat, ear infections, a staph infection, and this went on for six years. I did whatever it took to advocate for the health of my child, seen by an allergist, an ear-nose-and-throat doctor, and infectious disease experts. They had his blood drawn, and the blood test gave us answers. I vividly remember the doctor's call with the blood test results. That call brought relief to years of sickness, and a solution. With a revaccinating of the pneumococcal vaccine, the sickness stopped. Being intentional about my child's health, I mapped out the professionals he needed to be seen by, logged his sickness patterns, and focused on achieving our goal of finding answers, which led to a healthy child.

Life's journey isn't easy, and things don't always unfold as we envision. What I have come to know is when my confidence is shaken, I must choose to remain focused on making moves that get me closer to my end goal. I did that with graduate school, with my son's health, and my children's education as they graduated from IEP services. We spent many extra hours working on their speech, reading flash cards, and driving to services over the lunch hour and then returning to school, and many evenings in speech services. This dedication and early intervention led to a successful outcome of graduating from IEP services. These successful outcomes helped me see I could do the same with my career.

Move One: Switch careers. I jumped into a position where I was compensated based on my performance, which was riskier than my prior flat salary. This encouraged growth and a desire to develop as a leader. Accepting a role in banking, I began living outside my comfort zone. My mantra became "Get comfortable being uncomfortable." Each challenge I stretched beyond my comfort zone led to growth accompanied by rejection and lessons. For example, a peer once said to me, "Why do you choose to be a speaker when you are an expert of nothing?" Prior to 2017, I didn't have a business community, so it became a priority to build a support network. My superpower has always been building relationships and helping others. I brought my whole self to my meetings and began building a network of trusted peers. Within six months of hustling with back-to-back meetings, *St. Louis Small Business Monthly* named me one of the best business bankers in the region.

This was the first award my organization had ever received from this publication. Choosing to make an impact in my community made me a trusted advisor. The moment I realized who I wanted to become professionally in 2017, I created habits to support my desired outcome, set a positive mindset to overcome rejection, and took calculated risks. In 2022, I accepted the role as a health and benefits producer working for one of the world's largest insurance firms, which support most of the Fortune 500 companies in our country. After one month of being hired, I secured a new designation and jumped right in as a health and benefits consultant. As I continue to evolve, rejection is part of life; but it is when we accept challenges to push ourselves outside our comfort zone that we reach new levels. No longer do I allow fear to influence my decisions.

Move Two: Commit to professional development courses. "Intentional living is about living your best story," wrote John Maxwell. I commit to pick one professional development course each year to grow as a leader. The first self-development was a one-day, eight-hour course on Strategic Thinking, which, the next year, led me to taking a two-day, fifteen-hour course called Daring to Lead by Brené Brown. This course led me the following year to complete a three-month course called Women in Leadership by Focus St Louis, which led me to tackling a six-month course the following year called Leadership St Louis, also by Focus St Louis.

Each course, I grew personally, becoming more self-aware about defining my purpose and growing as a leader. These courses helped me own who I was. I began doing so by creating a place to turn hardships into hope by publishing my first anthology, *Owning Your G.R.I.T.* By being challenged, intimidated, and feeling like a fish out of water, I grew in the discomfort. This yearly habit of taking professional development courses gradually made me feel more equipped for lengthier challenges. This is an example of layering habits with reward, which I built into my routine.

Move Three: Engage in the community. I started serving by saying "yes" when others asked for help. This opened many doors, from participating on fundraising committees for nonprofits like Wings of Hope, to chairing the American Heart Association Cycle Nation Event and raising $30K. A servant leader, I received the National Volunteer of the Year Award on behalf of the AGCMO and made the cover of *St Louis Small Business Monthly*. In the past six years I have supported industries like technology, construction, manufacturing, higher education, nonprofits, and government. I am proud to say that I have volunteered numerous hours into my community and helped many. A mantra I live by is, "Be that person you needed during your darkest times." In my darkest times I needed community and support, which is why I founded G.R.I.T. Community, a free women's group supporting more than eight hundred women.

The commitment I made to myself gave me confidence discovering my passion and led to outcome such as advanced titles, awards, and community recognition. In six intense years of focusing on my career, I gradually advanced professionally, which shaped me into the leader I am today. What do you need to become more intentional about? Is it health, is it your professional development, developing a support network, or advancing in your career? Anything is possible if you implement strategic thinking, focus, habits, and if you remember that progress is gradual.

You may be on the wrong or right boat, but only you know. Who will you be in five, ten, and thirty years from today? You get to choose to jump off the boat and go for a swim, drive your boat, or ride through life as a passenger, but you have the power to choose and navigate your life. I chose to cut the strings attached to the bricks that had drowned my aspirations. I chose to swim when I switched industries twice, and I am now driving my own boat. When I listened to my internal compass in 2017, it encouraged me to jump in the driver's seat of my boat and evolve into who I envisioned. How will you begin to live your life with more intention?

Jennifer Bardot, MA, MS, is a publisher of the *Deconstructing GRIT Collection (GROWTH, RESILIENCE)* and *Owning Your G.R.I.T.*—all three international bestselling anthology books are available at Barnes & Noble and Walmart. She is featured on the cover of *St. Louis Small Business Monthly* as 2021's 100 St. Louisans You Should Know to Succeed in Business and was awarded the President's Circle by Enterprise Bank & Trust. Founder of the GRIT Community—a free women's leadership group—Jennifer holds certificates in the Dare to Lead Training by Brené Brown, Women in Leadership Class of '72, and Leadership St. Louis by Focus St. Louis. She serves Lindenwood University, Washington University, and Fontbonne University. Jennifer is passionate about supporting business owners and female leaders, and is a dedicated mother, community connector, and outdoor adrenaline adventurer.

Dr. Karen Hall

Educating for Change

"By demonstrating excellence in whatever skin we wear, we challenge ignorance by our very existence." —Adam Howard

I'll never forget the day I spent with my Aunt Imelda in her kindergarten classroom. I was four years old, and the visit was magical and fascinating. I loved every moment of what school looked like, even the smells. I thought the smell of milk was putrid. To this day, I'm not that fond of milk. Even though it was an unpleasant experience, I remember the milk carton, and ever since have associated the smell of milk in a carton with that memory. I was the guest student; I felt so special and proud. All the students had their eyes on me, and I loved being the focus of everyone's curiosity. I was allowed to sit at my auntie's desk and draw with the fat markers with the delicious fragrance associated with each color (purple smelled like grapes; that was my favorite. And black smelled like licorice, which was my least favorite).

From my seat in the corner of the classroom, I had a clear view of all the students and how they behaved. I was amazed at how mesmerized the students were by my auntie, and of their love for her. I didn't think any other place could be as loving as my home. Yet, in Aunt Imelda's classroom,

I discovered that my auntie was also an auntie to her students. I will never forget the impression of my Aunt Imelda while she was teaching.

As a Black woman, vital life experiences influenced me to become an educator. The strong Black women in my family encouraged and inspired me along my professional journey. I was fortunate to have models of female excellence and strength close to me. My Aunt Imelda and her sisters taught me valuable life lessons that have stayed with me. They fostered a love of learning and pushed me to reach my full potential. Their guidance and support ignited the fire in me to become an educator so that I could pay forward the gift of learning and a sense of belonging to others.

I grew up in the suburbs of St. Louis, Missouri. My experience was unique, however, as my neighborhood was a historically Black community called North Webster, my mother's hometown. We moved to my mother's childhood community in the middle of my kindergarten year. My child-hood was insulated with love and joy; I had a true sense of belonging in that close-knit community. People in the neighborhood remembered my mother when she and her siblings were young. Several generations of families remained in the area, a consequence of racial segregation years ago. As we know, segregation created numerous detrimental effects on Black people. As in many Black communities across the country, however, the people of North Webster made a way to thrive in those circumstances. Families found a way to educate their children regardless of inequitable resources and access.

My great aunties greatly impacted my socialization and view of what it meant to be a Black woman. Their commitment to their commu-nity and the children they educated was remarkable and affected our entire family. During the Depression, my great-grandparents somehow educated all nine of their children! My grandfather and his siblings were college graduates and set the family standard for learning, perseverance, and excellence. Earning a college degree in the family was not a dream but an expectation. The seven siblings in that family were teachers, so I was surrounded by intelligent and confident women. I was particularly close to my Aunt Imelda, the kindergarten teacher, and I treasure her name as my own middle name. It wasn't until I went to school and started kindergarten that I learned my racial identity carried a legacy of pain and suffering, the opposite of what my family, friends, and community instilled in me.

Before moving to St. Louis, I started kindergarten in Decatur, Illinois, where I completed the first half of the school year. I was so excited about starting kindergarten, and all my worries were put to rest because I had already experienced a kindergarten class with my Aunt Imelda. I was an expert and wanted to help other students. It only made sense to me that my first "real" schoolteacher would be like my auntie. But in the early weeks of school, I had a conflict with a fellow white student that ended badly with him calling me the "N" word. At age five, I didn't know the word's meaning, but I could tell by the student's facial expression and tone that he wanted to hurt my feelings. As a result, I ran to the teacher and reported what happened. Her response made an indelible mark on my spirit for the rest of my life. The teacher's face turned red, then I was told to ignore him. That's it. There was no explanation from the teacher, or any consequence given to the student. Unfortunately, I continued to have issues with that student until my time there ended and we moved to St. Louis.

During my time in elementary and secondary schools, I often didn't see myself reflected in the curriculum or the teachers who taught me. I rarely saw Black teachers in my classrooms, and the books we read rarely featured characters who looked like me. One of the most powerful lessons that my Aunt Imelda taught me was the importance of representation. First and foremost, she would tell me that being a Black teacher meant being intentional about understanding students' unique challenges. Aunt Imelda said that, as a Black woman, she had endured discrimination and prejudice firsthand in our society. Aunt Imelda knew her students experienced similar challenges. She felt her responsibility was to create a space where her students felt seen, heard, and valued.

As a young woman in my early twenties, I finally made it to that moment where I would have my own classroom. I went through all the necessary training, the practicums, and the planning to finally get to graduation. Early in my career, I understood that starting school with the right tone impacted the rest of the year. I wanted to intentionally create a classroom culture that prioritized respect and empathy. I instinctively wanted to encourage my students to share their thoughts and opinions, even if they disagreed. I wanted to teach them to listen to each other with an open mind and heart. I was determined to create a classroom culture where my students, from day one, would learn and grow together, treating each other with kindness and compassion.

I loved my classroom, room 303. I set up my room with care by putting up curtains and creating detailed lesson plans, took my position seriously, and intentionally thought about how to meet the needs of my students. When it finally came to "game day," my students arrived. I realized that not only did I want to be like my aunties, but I carried that crucial responsibility of representing as a Black teacher. I had arrived— I was becoming my Aunt Imelda.

One of the most important lessons I learned while teaching is the power of education to create change. Education can transform individuals and entire societies. Through education, we can challenge the status quo, dismantle systems of oppression, and create a more just and equitable world. As an educator, I see myself as a change agent. I strive to create learning opportunities that encourage critical thinking, problem-solving, and social responsibility. Our educators are responsible for teaching our students' academic subjects and the skills and values they need to be active and engaged citizens. By doing so, we can inspire them to become agents of change in their communities and beyond. I am grateful for the inspiration of my amazing Aunt Imelda. I understand the importance of being intentional in my approach to education. While being an educator is not easy, creating a more just and equitable society is essential. I am proud to be part of a community of educators working to make a difference.

To be intentional about creating a more just and equitable society: Stop. Think. Reflect.

1. How did race play a role in your childhood and/or adolescence? What impact did your family play in your cultural identity?

2. Think of a moment when your racial and cultural identity were important and manifested meaning to you and others.

3. How does your past influence your perception of racial issues and conversations?

4. Are you willing to be uncomfortable?

Dr. Karen I. Hall is an educational consultant, university assistant professor, and executive coach with extensive experience educating, advocating, and guiding action-focused conversations centered around the theory, practice, and business of equity-focused leadership. She has been instrumental in assessment forecasting, analysis, and strategic planning for academic initiatives while mentoring, coaching, and supporting educators to ensure professional development and equity-focused student progress. She started as a teacher and continued her career in educational administration, including building-level administration and central services, and recently retired as superintendent.

As an educational consultant, Dr. Hall has an extended platform for delivering equity-focused leadership through numerous public presentations, community-based consultations, and the acquisition and development of superintendents nationwide. She continually advocates for diversity and inclusion at the forefront of every educational endeavor by forging innovative community awareness initiatives, cultivating trusted relationships, and directing organizations to adopt inclusive methodologies.

Roberta Moore

The Call That Changed My Life

What do you do when you receive the phone call you've been dreading and expecting for most of your adult life? I am agonizing over this question as I'm standing in front of my office refrigerator, on a cold sunny day, at lunchtime in Hendersonville, North Carolina. I just finished with my 11:00 a.m. client and am rushing to get my lunch because there is just one hour to eat, return phone calls, jump on the trampoline, and center myself before the 1:00 p.m. client. My cell phone blinks in my right hand with a voicemail from my youngest sister asking me to call her. My visceral sense tells me her request is urgent.

I call her back as I stand in front of the refrigerator, not bothering to take the time to walk back to my desk. Before I hear my sister's voice, I already know what she is going to say. Our sister is dead. It appears she's taken her own life. She rigged a hose from the exhaust pipe of her car into the passenger seat, closed the car window and the garage door, and turned on the ignition. Do we know exactly what happened next? Did my sister say the car was still running when someone found her? I start to wonder how much time had passed while she lay there dead before someone found her. Who did my sister say found her body? Did she say there was a suicide note? My brain locks up, and nothing more is registering in this moment.

Her death remains shrouded in mystery. My surviving sister emailed me the suicide note, but when I read it, most of it didn't make much sense. I knew from my psychology training that when people commit suicide, they are temporarily insane and not thinking clearly. To take your own life is incongruent with our human instinct to survive. I don't know why my sister made her decision, and this dark news still haunts me. I think part of her did want to live because she had just purchased new clothing and a puppy one hour before her death. Why would she do that if she was also planning to die?

But this much I know: a part of me was relieved to hear that news. It signaled an end to the constant distress running in my unconscious mind because I never knew when my mother would call and tell me about some new tragedy in my sister's life. Because I had complained during childhood that my sister needed professional help, my mother often accused me of not loving my sister or having enough empathy for her. Nothing was farther from the truth, but I could never prove that to my mother or either of my sisters. I made efforts to understand and connect with my sister, but we were distant. I felt powerless in this chronic struggle. The moment I heard the news about my sister's death was life-changing for obvious reasons and yet it became worse over time. It became the beginning of losing what little was left of the relationships I had with my mother and surviving sister.

Despite the distance between us, my sister's death inspired me to set a powerful intention that changed the trajectory of my life. I'd like to share this transformation with you now. Setting clear, purposeful, and heartfelt intentions can mean the difference between a life that is well lived and one that is rudderless.

After speaking with my sister, I stayed at work and saw all my afternoon and evening clients. I didn't want to cancel anyone. I needed the structure and routine of work to help me feel grounded and soothed. Although I compartmentalized the searing news of my sister's suicide, it continued to work through my heart. I was more open and affected by my clients' stories than usual, in a way that made me feel raw and authentically connected to them. I was so open that my intuition was on extra-high alert. My sensitivity made me feel more emotionally present, and the sessions felt vitally important. As the workday ended, I went to the bathroom and vomited out all the negatively charged thoughts that I'd held throughout the day.

Weeks later, I was concerned that my continuing to work the day I got the news was maladaptive behavior. Then I remembered that there isn't one right way to cope with grief. Everyone copes in their own way. Even the famous psychiatrist Carl Jung, whom I greatly admire, continued to work without taking a break when he was grieving an important loss in his life. As the days passed, I did my best to process my feelings and live with the news. I felt changed and different in a way that felt both disturbing and life-affirming.

I had to surrender to the fact that I had no control over the choices my mother and surviving sister made as they decided how to wrap up my sister's life. (This is a pattern in my family that I do not like or understand: my mother chooses not to have funerals nor publish obituaries.) There would be no formal, public closure. I sought my own way to honor my sister's life. One day while driving to Spartanburg, South Carolina, I found it.

I am a member of a "Dream Group" of psychotherapists who meet at Converse University to discuss and analyze nighttime dreams. I love this group, and meetings feel like sacred time apart from my everyday world. As I parked and got ready to go into the building, I got the chills. I heard my sister's voice in my mind, telling me that she was safe, happy, and okay.

She told me to go on about my life and to cherish what I have. As I shared this with the women in my group, it became even more real and significant. In that moment, I set my intention to live every day of my life to the fullest, because my sister's life was cut short.

The next miraculous moment happened inside the Sisters of the Pauline Bookstore on King Street in Charleston, South Carolina. As I shopped the religious jewelry, I was once again overcome by chills and the sensation of my sister being present in my mind. I decided to purchase a beautiful silver Mother Mary Miraculous Medal, which hung from a silver chain necklace. This became my next intention: to wear this necklace as a reminder to live my life to the fullest, because my sister could not choose that.

Later that week, my husband and I attended Saturday evening mass at Charleston's St. John the Baptist Cathedral. Again, chills came as the priest said in his homily that even at the last moment of life, when someone asks God for forgiveness, they instantly have it. I started crying, and I believed that this is what happened for my sister. As I listened to the priest, I remembered the time years ago when I prayed to get hit by a car so I wouldn't have to intentionally end my own life. I was young, lonely, and feeling hopeless. I wanted to die just to end the emotional pain. The very next day, I was crossing the street to go to church and almost got hit by a car because I wasn't paying attention. Startled, I thanked God then and there that my prayer went unanswered. I wondered why I had those dark thoughts like my sister did. The saying "there but for the grace of God go I" fits for me because, at one time, I was close to feeling what my sister might have felt.

I realized then that my sister and I were similar but different. At the time I said that dark prayer, I did not have the strong faith I had that day when hearing the news of my sister's suicide. I built my faith by going to therapy, studying psychology, writing in journals as a way of examining my life, analyzing my dreams, praying, and setting intentions to be the very best version of myself that I could possibly be.

My quest is human and never-ending. We create our own life stories. How we narrate those stories is relevant and meaningful. I did not like the story I was telling myself, so I prayed to God to help me see things differently. God's response helped me set another intention.

I blamed my mother and sisters for the pain of feeling rejected. During morning meditation and prayer time, I began to visualize sending love to my family, even on days I wasn't feeling it. I kept this intention almost daily until I felt the burden of my own negative narratives lift and transform. I affirm daily that I am the only human responsible for how my life unfolds. We can transform any dark thought through the fierce intention of love, forgiveness, and understanding.

EQ-i Coach founder, executive coach, and author of *Emotion at Work: Unleashing the Secret Power of Emotional Intelligence*, Roberta Moore draws on nearly four decades in executive coaching, professional services, and psychotherapy to help her clients understand and unleash the power of emotional intelligence (EQ) through individual and team EQ coaching, team workshops, and EQ assessments and audits. Moore's work earned her a 2020 Enterprising Women of the Year Award, one of the most prestigious recognitions for women business owners, as well as a 2020 Globee Women World Female Achievers Champion of the Year Award and a 2021 Stevies Award. Moore is also a member of the Forbes Coaches Council and publishes monthly articles in *Forbes*. She is a contributing author to the 2020 book *The Anatomy of Accomplishment: Your Guide to Bigger, Better, Bolder Business Results*, an anthology of professional wisdom from women business leaders across the country.

Taryn Pulliam

A Path of My Own

My life has been filled with intention, even when I was a young adult. I chose to leave home at eighteen years of age. The choice made things more difficult than they needed to be. In my young arrogance, I thought no one was going to tell me what to do, so I left. It was not because life was terrible, because it wasn't. I lived in a comfortable home where my mom loved and supported me. She guided me toward a college path and helped me create a roadmap to a successful future. Driving back to school after Thanksgiving break during my first semester, I got into a car accident. As the doctors treated my injuries, we discovered by chance that I had congenital emphysema. Two months later, the lower two lobes of my right lung were removed. This experience changed the trajectory of my life. I was nineteen years old.

When I woke up from the surgery, my throat hurt. The pain was from the air tube that had been not so gingerly placed by a student doctor. Also, I had black, blue, and purple bruises up and down my arms, since the anesthesiologist was also a student. My chest cavity ached, and I felt the sting of the tubes that were inserted just beneath my skin with every move. Sitting in a hospital, with a huge, ugly, painful scar and two tubes draining blood and fluid out of my side, I broke down. While recovering, one thoughtless doctor told me I probably wouldn't live past fifty-five years of age, and that was scary. He was wrong, but at that time I set my intention: "If I am going to die, I am going to live it up and not focus on this cookie-cutter path that others want for me."

I quit college and started down a different path that led me to working in the service industry and eventually cosmetology school. Believe it or not, I am skilled at color and cuts and can make your hair look beautiful! Working in this industry, however, I was missing something. For one thing, the benefits were not that great, and there was no 401(k). By this time, I'd figured out I was probably not dying at fifty-five, or even seventy-five, because the women in my family live well into their nineties. This revelation came with getting sick one too many times, and not being able to get Z-Pak medication when I needed it. My health journey brought me some much-needed maturity.

I decided it was time to get back to college. This time I lived on my own and had all the bills that came with it. That meant working full time while going to school full time. This would seem like a lot to most people, but I felt like I was behind, so I attended Lindenwood University's accelerated program. This period of my life was filled, as Rihanna says, with "work, work, work, work, work!" I got it done with Intention. My schedule consisted of wake up, gym time, work, school, homework, sleep, and repeat. Luckily, I had taken some courses in high school and some college before my accident, and a few classes here and there, so I was able to graduate from Lindenwood in about three years with my Human Resources (HR) Management degree.

I was so excited and ready to start my future. I started applying for jobs. In HR they want you to have two years of experience, but no one wants to hire you without experience. The only jobs I found did not pay well and would not have been even a third of what I made in the service industry. Add to that my student loan payments, and things were looking dismal to say the least.

A friend of mine offered to get me an interview at the company he worked for, but it would most likely be an administrative job. The company had good insurance and great benefits, so I thought, "What I have got to lose?" At the interview, I was introduced to one of the sales managers I would support. The conversation quickly turned to my customer service experience and how confident I seemed talking to people. The interview lasted three hours. Later, the manager told me, "Sales is hard." There was a reason he'd kept me in the interview for so long. Most people would have been frustrated after an hour, but I kept a positive attitude through the process, and I got the job. Not the admin job, but the account manager job!

Most of the account managers there got a territory with several zip codes. I was given one and was told I had to prove myself. Later, the same manager who hired me told me I should wear dresses. Dresses?? The president did not like me because I had stripes in my hair. We call those highlights where I come from. I asked the manager if he'd read my resumé. Did he see my degree was in HR Management? He was well intentioned, and I think of him as a great mentor, but I left that day, got in my car, and called my mom. I was so angry, I was in tears. My mother, who is quite an accomplished educator, said, "Taryn, you can cry and quit, or you can be the best salesperson in the company." She was right. I decided that I was going to be so disciplined and intentional with my goals that no one could stop me. By December they gave me a full territory, and since I'd started in August, that made me proud. I stayed with that company for another three years and achieved the President's Club Award every year.

This was only half my story, however. Remember those pesky student loans? I decided that I did not want them lingering around the rest of my life. So, while I worked my sales job during the day, I also worked two nights and weekends at a salon. Remember that I went to cosmetology school? Well, since I was single and had more free time than someone who was married, I worked. I was used to the super-busy schedule. I decided to be intentional with that time while I had the energy and freedom to work hard and pay off what I owed. I wanted to be debt free for life.

Since I was successful in sales, people could not believe that I was working two jobs. I enjoyed both jobs for different reasons. Sales invigorated my mind. I liked the hustle and helping people find solutions that improved their business. I enjoyed the salon because when my clients left, they felt good about themselves. I helped them feel beautiful. As Maya Angelou says, "…people will forget what you did, but people will never forget how you made them feel." Both professional experiences have shaped me into the businesswoman I am today.

Fast-forward seven years. I eventually paid off my student loans. The great feeling I had was my reward for intentionally working to pay off the debt I owed. Funny thing about working at the salon? I met a lot of great people there. When I got married, my husband said he wanted me to quit because I no longer had to juggle everything, and I had a partner to help and support my goals. He was right. But after my seven-year, two-job journey, I felt kind of lazy. I was so used to going a hundred miles an hour, normal pace felt like I was failing. I had to learn that it is OK to slow down.

By this time, I was back selling for the company I had previously worked for. I was a success, making President's Club and going on trips, but I found I was hungry for more. I realized I would not have the opportunity with this company to achieve my goals and ambitions. It was time for a change. Interestingly enough, a client from the salon reached out to me and told me the great organization she worked for was hiring. She recommended me to them, saying I was the real deal and a hard worker. She knew both sides of me. She spoke so highly of this place that I knew

I had to apply. After a few interviews and a few weeks, I got the job. It is an amazing place to work.

During this journey, I have learned a lot. The diagnosis I received at nineteen changed my vision for the path I would take in life. Most would say it was the hard way; and while it was certainly not the way the world says you should achieve success, it was my own path, and I learned that hard work pays off. Communication and authentic connections improve chances of success. Setting goals and not giving up allows you to accomplish almost anything. Operating in humility and bringing the best version of yourself, no matter where you show up to work, builds character. I may have pieced together my cookie instead of using the world's cutter, but boy is my life sweet.

Taryn Pulliam is the Senior Director of Strategic Partnerships at Gadell-Net Consulting Services. She has been with GadellNet since 2019. Taryn has more than twenty years of experience in business development. She specializes in cultivating new relationships and finding strategic partners who believe in their core values of 100 percent accountability, zero excuses, make an impact, and a grow or die philosophy. Taryn creates her customers' vision of their personal experience.

Taryn also sits on the board for Covenant House Missouri. This organization welcomes youth who are runaway, trafficked, at-risk, or experiencing homelessness, and they do with unconditional love, absolute respect, and a place to call home. Taryn is passionate about helping youth move from homelessness to hope.

She has been married for ten years and has a wonderful son. Her family and faith in God keep her focused on building strong relationships, continuous growth, and compassion for others.

Debi Corrie

Taking Intentional Risks

It was May 2020, and I was excited to attend a virtual online event. It promised to help business owners break through their glass ceilings. It had a proven process to help them achieve their goals. It was a three-day event, and I had cleared my calendar to attend. One of the guest speakers was Barbara Cochran, one the of Sharks from ABC's *Shark Tank* series. My intention was to learn information at this three-day seminar that I could take back to my clients. As an avid learner, I was always looking for new ways to help them grow their businesses.

By the end of the seminar, I wound up joining the organization. It offered coaching, masterminding, and a plan that helped business owners create companies that were self-sufficient. I had mixed emotions of excitement and fearfulness. What if it didn't work? Even more scary was: What if it did? Little did I realize that this was the first step on a journey toward my life's work.

My first coaching session was in May. I looked forward to meeting my coach for the first time. It was an opportunity to hear from an outsider how I could grow my practice. That meeting changed my life and my business forever. The pandemic had taken a toll on some of my clients and made me realize that I had to do things differently to help them succeed. At the time, I was the partner at another organization where each partner ran their own practice, had their own clients, and the organization for support. My coach asked me what my goals were for my business. It was simple: I wanted to help business owners and create a company with a seven-figure income.

The next words he said sent me into a tailspin. "You know with the current setup, the most you can earn is the mid-six figures." It took me by surprise, because I had never considered that working alone in running my practice would have such an impact on my goals. To grow a business, I would need a team. The current organization I was working for did not allow partners to hire employees to expand their practices. The work had to be done by each partner individually. We ended the call, and I had some serious thinking and decision-making to do.

Like many people, the pandemic taught me some valuable lessons. The services we provided to business owners were not an hourly commodity. My worth was not just in the hours of service I provided to clients, but in the strategy and experiences I brought to the table to help them increase cash flow and generate better profits. Although I had been expanding my practice, I had not been doing it with intention and thought. My life was caught up in the day-to-day functions of my business. One of the first questions I ask new clients is, "What is your vision for the next three to five years?" To be successful, I had to answer this question for myself.

What was the vision that I had to help people in the business world? Zoom made it possible to work effectively with clients virtually now. No longer did I need to be limited to a geographical area. I knew the hourly model of work prevented some clients from reaching out with questions on important matters. How could I help more business owners and get fairly compensated in the process?

While answering these questions, I realized that the way I did business had to change. The partners I worked with were amazing, but my goals had changed. My heart was helping smaller business owners in eight figures or less obtain their business goals. In June of 2022, the idea for a new business was born.

The next meeting with my coach had a big impact on me. "So Debi, what are we going to cover today?" my coach asked. I responded, "Well, I have been doing a lot of thinking about what you said in our last meeting, and you are right. I can't reach my goals under my current practice. I am going to go out under my own umbrella. I am writing a book, *Loving Failure: Getting Control of Your Business Health*" and have signed with a publisher to launch the book in November along with my company." My coach's response: "Let's lock and load!" Thinking through my vision made me be more intentional with my business and goals.

I had wanted to write and publish the book for a long time. It was meant to be a helpful guide to both business owners who were new to business and those that had been established. Finance can be such a hard topic because it has a language all its own. My goal was to speak in plain English, and share stories, hints, and fails with business owners. It would be a reference for them when they wanted to learn how to use finance to create a better business.

Writing the book and launching the business in November were not the hardest things I had yet to do. The reason I left the partnership was to be able to hire employees and expand my business to reach more clients. That was the purpose: hire people to reach more business owners. That first hire was terrifying. Many business owners experience this when hiring their first employee. I was scared because, for the first time, I would be responsible for another person and their family and to make sure that the business was growing. I would have payroll. It was the first of many times that I would have to walk into my fear with intention and believe that it would work.

That first employee was my executive assistant. She took all the day-to-day tasks that were not revenue-producing off my plate. That one hire helped me double my business the first year. It helped me start a business that would help business owners with CFO strategy, accounting, taxes, and tax planning. We hired accountants and analysts to help us. Our third year the business grew another 60 percent. We were on the fast track.

There are so many fears when you own a business. You never know what the future holds. You don't know where your next customer will come from. Employees come and go. Clients come and go. Sometimes these issues keep you awake at night as you navigate business ownership. I wanted to create a culture of giving for employees who wanted to come to work every day. To do that I had to get more purposeful with my intentions and vision.

My vision is to help business owners be successful. Successful business owners create great employee cultures and contribute to their communities by providing employment. Those employees and owners can then contribute to their communities and create a culture where people help each other, in self-sustaining communities that create environments where people want to work, live, and play. Intention.

Living a life of intention is about knowing what you want and figuring out what you need to get there. My mother has taught me many valuable lessons in life. If you want something bad enough, you can make it happen. As a leader, it is your job to figure out how to make things happen. Leaders do not have to have all the answers, but they need to act and make decisions. Having a team and letting them know your vision and intention creates a company where people share your vision and want to make things happen.

Intention is the willingness to walk into your fear and be willing to fail. Intention is making decisions, even when they are not popular. Intention is the power behind the actions to make things happen. Knowing where you want to be is the magic sauce to getting where you want to go. Intention does not need to know the how and the what, just the why. The how and what will work itself out. Intention is the word that describes how to live a fulfilled life.

Debi Corrie is the owner and CEO of Acumaxum, a strategic CFO company. Acumaxum helps business owners increase cash, maximize profits, and scale their businesses. She owns two other companies. Taxpertise LLP is a tax strategy company with a partner, and DJC Media is her personal publishing company.

She is a #1 bestselling author of *Loving Failure: Getting Control of Your Business Health*. She is a motivational guest speaker on various topics. She has been featured on CBS News, NBC, Fox, and in the *Boston Herald*, *Market Watch*, and *Star Tribune*. Debi is a St. Louis Titan 100 for 2023 and has received other local recognition.

Debi received her Bachelor of Science degree in Business Administration with a major in Accounting from the University of Missouri–St Louis. She is a CPA, CGMA, and a member of the American Institute of Certified Public Accountants (AICPA), and the National Association of Tax Professionals (NATP).

Angela Pinon

Intention – Education – Celebration

Graduation Day! A day of reflection and celebration. My children, along with all the rest of my family, were present to celebrate this day with me. I was the first in my family to earn a college degree. I cried tears of joy; I just could not contain them. Such a huge accomplishment and wonderful experience to be able to share with my children. Watching the smiles on their faces and feeling their joy and excitement as we heard my name being called and I walked across the stage to be presented with my Bachelor of Science in Accounting. So much emotion all around me and within me was quite the experience for sure. My children knew firsthand the hard work and sacrifice it took to get there, and now they were seeing the payoff. I was beyond excited, and I felt so accomplished. That moment was the realization of the powerful intention I set for myself when I became a mother.

My whole world changed the day I became a mom. My perception of life changed. I realized I was wholly responsible for the lives of my children, as well as myself. The person I was, the beliefs I had, and ultimately my overall perception of even my own life experiences all changed in what seemed like the blink of an eye. I had to take a moment, step back, and reevaluate my life: where it was going, how I intended to change it, and how I would get there.

Being a mom, I had to continue working hard to better myself so I could provide for my children. I wanted so much more for my children than I had, and I wanted them to have better life experiences and more opportunities than I had available to me. Every life choice I made along the way was difficult, and I alone was tasked to weigh the consequences of the decisions I made and continue to make. I prayed for guidance and read a ton of books. Many times, these decisions involved personal sacrifice, but the benefits to my children's lives always made it worthwhile. To tell the truth, I really had no idea how to parent my children, and the fact that I had to do it on my own, based on what I had learned, was a real challenge. For this reason, education and personal growth and development became an integral part of my everyday life. My intention became (and remains) to provide the best possible life for my children through my continuing education and development.

It took me more years to earn my college degree than I would like to admit, but it was so worth it. I began taking classes way back when my children first started elementary school—one class at a time over the years with a few breaks in between for life events. I managed to raise my children, provide for them, and be a part of their lives while balancing a full-time career and attending my classes late into the night. I admit, there were some classes I cried through, and some sleepless nights too; but it paid off in the end. I went on to earn my master's for Business Administration, while at the same time assisting my two oldest children as they prepared to graduate from high school and head for college themselves.

By living my life this way, guided by intentional life choices defined by my values and responsibilities, I helped further develop my children's values and character. I was not just preaching the importance of education; I was demonstrating it (with intention). I did not have to preach work ethic, or sacrifice now for a better tomorrow, or responsibility, because they observed me living it firsthand. And because I shared my goals (my intentions) with my children, they absorbed the value of goal setting and of staying true to that which you define as important.

They have learned the importance of education and personal growth and development and why it is Number One in our home. I intentionally raised them with the belief that education and personal growth and development can and should always be a part of their everyday lives.

My children are now young adults and making their own life decisions. They have developed their own beliefs and values with a little guidance from me over the course of their lives. While I don't always agree with every choice they make, I am proud of their value systems and respect their life choices. Many times, we have celebrated their accomplishments together, and I am especially proud when their own intention, coupled with hard work and commitment, results in them achieving more than they thought possible. For as long as I can, I will be here to support them with anything they may need. Because they are grown, I can now focus a little more on myself and what is best for me. This is allowing me the opportunity to expand further into my own personal growth and development.

I wake up every morning, have my cup of coffee, and plan out my day. I think about what it is I need and want, and sometimes I even create the infamous to-do list, and then organize and prioritize accordingly. I have learned, over time, how important it is to give myself some flexibility so I can improvise and adapt to changes and events throughout my day. My lists almost always include some type of continuing education or social networking and a little time for myself. Some projects I take on extend over several months while others may be only an hour or two. I set out with intention to improve my management skills, and last year I earned the prestigious Cornell University Diversity, Equity & Inclusion Certification.

I have made those values and practices a part of my everyday business life. This year I have been working on Nonprofit Accounting and Management Certifications through the AICPA (American Institute of Certified Public Accounting) to advise and serve those clients more effectively.

I lead the Client Accounting and Advisory Services Team at Schmersahl Treloar CPA's. The firm's managing partner, Jim Schmersahl, has been and continues to be an incredible mentor. I am so grateful for the knowledge and the many opportunities that have blessed me. It not only benefits me but my staff and clients as well. Even as I lead the professionals on my team, I grow and benefit from them as we work together to add value for our clients. I believe my team has learned from me; I know I have grown from knowing and working with each one of them.

It is my intention to continue to balance work and my personal life in a way that makes me happy. One of my personal value-added goals is to give back to my community. I achieved this by dedicating my time to both working with and volunteering for one of our firm's clients, Pedal the Cause, in helping them to Create a World Without Cancer.

Like me, you may already be living a life of intention, you are just not aware of it or have not given it much thought. Intentional living comes from living out your personal values, staying true to the true you. When was the last time you stopped to think about your core values? You should. Today. Then act to reflect those values in your daily activities. Our beliefs, life experiences, actions, and decisions that are important to us individually all help to shape and cultivate our personal core values. I have been blessed with many meaningful life experiences (and challenges), and with intention I have taken the lessons learned from those experiences and incorporated them into the fabric of my life.

Living with intention has helped me tune out those everyday noises that conspire to distract from what is important. It is a mindset that defines and enriches my life. I have come to understand and appreciate what it means to live a life of intention and be the best me that I can be. I did not call it intention at first; it was simply my focused, driven purpose, born of the need to be better, and thus to build a better life for me and my children. In turn, we have celebrated many of my children's accomplishments over the years, and I am so proud to see the ways they live their values and goals with intention.

My life is more fulfilling and impactful because I live every day with intention, and I intend to continue.

Angela Pinon is the Client Accounting & Advisory Services Manager for Schmersahl Treloar, CPA's. She has more than twenty years of CPA-firm experience serving business and nonprofit clients. She combines her accounting expertise with varied industry and life experiences to develop and deliver practical business solutions for her clients. She is a dedicated mom, passionate about being a trusted advisor, a mentor to staff, and a thought leader in the firm.

Angela has earned her Bachelor of Science in Accounting and Master of Business Administration. She has achieved the designation Advanced Certified ProAdvisor in QuickBooks/QBO, and holds a certification in Diversity, Equity & Inclusion from Cornell University. She is a member of the American Institute of Certified Public Accountants, the Missouri Society of Certified Public Accountants, and the Institute of Management Accountants.

She gives of her time supporting Pedal the Cause in their mission to Create a World Without Cancer.

Kimberly Lebbing

Embracing the Storms

As long as I can remember, I have always been intrigued by storms. I felt there was something mystical and cleansing about them. I remember growing up on a farm and my grandmother telling me to pay attention to nature and how it gave us signs that a storm was coming. The leaves on the maple trees would turn up, just so . . . nature's whisper that a storm was on the way. I remember feeling afraid, but also internal excitement, knowing that the storm was blowing in. If we were paying attention, there would be time to prepare.

I don't know that I fully understood it at the time, but it was like I had an internal understanding that only the strong parts of everything would survive the storm. It would wash away what was dead and no longer needed. The storm had an intention: to cleanse and blow away, and also a deeper intention to promote growth. Growth always happens after a storm. Sometimes it's subtle growth; sometimes it is a total rebuild.

There are times in my life when facing my personal "storms" that I forgot this understanding. Because I was so focused on surviving the storm, I wasn't able to be intentional about becoming and being who I wanted to be. I didn't even understand what that meant. The storm left imprints on me. Imprints of subconscious filters that needed to be peeled away before I could have the clarity of being intentional. These personal storms revealed what needed to be washed and blown away, and, in some cases, totally rebuilt so that I could lead a life of true purpose and intention.

Throughout the majority of my life, I would allow whatever happened to me to just happen, and I became a victim of the storm. Blowing along wherever the wind took me. I didn't have a sense of intention or purpose and felt lost in my own personal storms.

One of my first storms was when I was about four years old. I was playing with my toys, listening to my childhood Disney story records, and just being and doing what little girls do. I would get lost for hours in my own little world, not really aware of what was going on outside of my playtime. I wasn't the best at picking things up when I was finished and wasn't even really sure or intentional that this was something that I needed to do. However, my dad was a very particular type of person. He liked to keep things orderly, clean, and tidy. He lost his temper when he saw the mess. It was an extreme reaction, and he often behaved this way throughout my childhood. I was constantly walking on eggshells and became extremely quiet and withdrawn because of it. In fact, I didn't talk to most people, even in school, because I was so terrified of saying or doing the wrong thing.

What I didn't understand back then was that he was one of the storms of my life. His temper raged just as much as a storm does, and it was over-powering when I was in the middle of it. Later, I would come to realize just how much these storms shaped who I am today. My storms led to several subconscious filters that I created in order to stay safe and protect myself.

These subconscious filters told me that it wasn't safe to play, that if I didn't do things right I would get in trouble, and that being quiet was much safer and easier than voicing any opinions. It also caused me to be extremely cautious and fearful of a lot of things, including making friends and having any kind of deep relationships.

As I grew into adulthood, this outlook prevented me from living life with intention. I came out of my shell a little with the help of counseling, and eventually met my husband and got married. At this point, I was still unaware that my behaviors and decisions were being created from my stormy past.

After our first child was born, I started my own business, mainly because I wanted the freedom to stay home with her and our future kids. I wanted time flexibility and all the perks of being a business owner, so that is what I set out to do. I tried several different businesses, thinking that if I could just find the right thing, I would be successful.

I quickly realized that it wasn't the businesses; it was me. I was my own worst enemy. I looked confident and successful on the outside, but on the inside I was constantly second-guessing myself. I would get to a certain level of success and then remain there, always looking for the next thing that would lift me up.

I was not aware of all the filters I had going on that were affecting my behaviors. There were many, to say the least. Conflicts about making money and being a good wife and mother, and feeling worthy and accepted. This was the case even after I had been through several years of counseling and personal growth.

I was constantly judging and calculating whether or not an action would be safe. It showed up very subtly. I wasn't aware of it, but there was a pause on just about everything I considered doing. I was constantly judging whether it would make me feel accepted and loved. Ultimately, I didn't trust or value myself.

It's interesting how these filters show up in your business and in your personal life. In my business, there was always an underlying fear of showing up fully because the internal filters were saying that it wasn't safe. Quite the opposite of living a life with intention, which, ironically, back then, I would have told you I was doing.

In relationships, I never really allowed anyone to get too close. If they did, there was the risk of being hurt or, ultimately, being judged about who I was. Again the storm brewed, along with the filters and the lack of intention. What I now know is that I was literally afraid to be me. Fully me. I knew there was something underneath, but never really allowed her to show up because I was constantly judging and calculating whether or not it would be safe.

For me, living a life of intention means that I am staying true to myself and showing up authentically, ignoring anything that doesn't align with my values and beliefs. Somewhere along the way, I started to imitate people who looked successful to me. I followed their advice and accomplished some goals, but something felt off. I knew I wasn't being true to my authentic self. Before long, I lost who I really was.

I believed that I was not good enough, not smart enough, and not strong enough to be truly successful. I was being intentional about success but wasn't intentional about who and how I was showing up in the world, and it left me searching for answers.

What I found was that even though I thought I had worked through those initial storms through lots of counseling and self-development programs, the gifts of the storm were hidden underneath the rubble and had been ignored for years. I learned how to cope, and thought I was getting along in life just fine, but I also knew that deep down more work was needed. More digging in and finding the gifts, and unearthing the true, authentic me.

During my "unearthing," I discovered that my filter of calculating everything was causing me to not really be in the moment. It's hard to be intentional when you are always thinking about the next thing. Shifting these internal filters was key to having a business and life that truly felt aligned.

I had to revisit the storms and dig through the rubble to find the gifts. There are parts of me that had to go through a total rebuild or transformation. I did this by focusing on my energy or how I was showing up in the world and connecting to my true self.

It goes against modern culture, but it's been my experience that when I slow down enough, I am able to be more intentional. Being intentional without all those subconscious filters that were bogging me down shifted the energy that I was showing up in. It made my business lighter and easier, and it made my relationships more meaningful. I now understand that the storm had an intention, and with it comes joy and great purpose.

Now, I help entrepreneurs shift their storms. To shift a personal storm, ask yourself, "What behavior or energy pattern is showing up?" If it's a pattern that's been there a while, it's likely linked to before age seven, when our subconscious is developed. Next, show yourself grace. You probably developed that pattern as a way to protect yourself. And lastly, find the gifts. They can transform into something beautiful.

Entrepreneurs seek Kimberly Lebbing's services to uncover their subconscious limitations because many feel out of alignment with their business or relationships and don't know why or how to shift it.

With her intuitive guidance, she empowers them to shift their energy from confusion to clarity, frustration to fulfillment, and to transform into a new energy so that their businesses and relationships become easier and lighter.

With over 796 hours of training, five expert-level certifications in Neurolinguistics-based Transformational Coaching, and fourteen top-level trainings from three different programs over the last eight years, she has studied and intuitively extracted the best elements to create her own proven process so that her clients can experience true transformation and alignment with their goals at a soul level.

Kimberly Lebbing is a wife to Mark, and a mother of three young adults. She loves the outdoors, traveling, and connecting with nature as much as possible.

Rachel Rubin Wilkins

G.O.A.L.
Go Out And Live!

In 2005, the sentence "Create Your BEST life, live with intent: INTEN-TION" spoke to me from a sage-green canvas art frame while shopping. The color scheme matched my house décor, but the words matched my personal mantra for most of my life. I had to buy it. Intentionality is a way of life and mindset for me. For years I have mapped out goals, jotted in journals, and plotted yearly calendars that forged plans, shaping my future and those around me. Goals, dreams, and visions have come true through the power of a positive mindset, determination, and perseverance. One of the most noteworthy phrases came from my dad, the king of intentions and living life to its fullest, as he always said, "The most important part of the day is a plan." Over the years, intentionality has surfaced through a daily plan in the major facets of my life: education, love, parenting, and my career.

Youthful Intentions

Known for being quite independent and adventurous, it was hard to visualize where my young self would land as an adult woman. The world was enormous and full of opportunities, and I wanted to experience them all. Living close to my preschool, my mom and I walked that route multiple times. On the walk to my first day of preschool, I turned to my mother at the corner and said, "It's okay, Mom, you can leave. I can take it from here." She was speechless.

As a mother of five, I know how proud and pained she must have felt. Her goal was to raise a strong, independent daughter. My four-year-old self was eager and excited to arrive at school. I was very intentional about making my mark on the world. Rooted deep within me, I knew I would grow, learn, and find my gifts in academic spaces. I was ready to Go Out And Live! Perhaps it was my intention to show the world I was big enough to handle my first day of preschool. Perhaps it was my subconscious yet intentional independent and adventurous spirit that surged forward to confidently explore this new stage of life. This spirited, courageous mindset would serve my future self well.

Focused on Education and Finding My Gifts

"If you can imagine it, you can achieve it. If you can dream it, you
can become it." – William Arthur Ward

Raised in St. Louis, I dreamt of attending the University of Missouri–Columbia. Multiple family members shared stories telling tall Tiger (our mascot) tales about "the good old days." In high school, I prepared and followed the challenging process for college admission. I set calculated goals to achieve this dream. On campus at MU, I intentionally seized the most out of my college days. I rose in leadership as a director of Homecoming, led many of MU's committees and organizations and worked throughout college, holding two to three jobs, graduating debt free.

Overwhelmed and excited by the variety of degree choices, I explored degrees in French, Education and Journalism. My Grandfather Litzsinger, a high school biology teacher, inspired this interest as he chaperoned summer study abroad programs. I have fond memories as a young girl of watching slideshows displaying his travels from a projector in the living room. Mesmerized and captivated, I dreamt that I, too, would chaperone programs and send postcards and photos from such places. After a summer studying abroad in Grenoble, France, I returned home a different person with a new focus. The trip sparked a love for international travel and fueled my passion to earn an Interdisciplinary Studies degree in Business Marketing, Sociology, and French. I sharpened my gifts, graduated debt free, and landed a job after graduation as a recruiter for the university. I found my gifts. I imagined it and I achieved it.

Intentional About Love

At Mizzou, I met my husband, and we spent the final years of college together. Our kids call us "college sweethearts." He received an Army ROTC scholarship, which meant he would serve four years in active duty after college. I was intentional about marrying a person who would show adventure, love, reliability, and grit through the toughest parts of life. We were about to embark on the challenges of the Army lifestyle. Intentionality played a huge part in our survival. As the saying goes, "Home was where the Army sent us." I learned to deeply cherish moments.

Life is not about perfection nor perfect people. It is about intentionally celebrating perfect moments: a snow-dusted military wedding surrounded by loved ones; the birth of five beautiful, smart children; the emotional embrace after eleven exhausting Army Ranger deployments; or the joyful bliss released watching our children graduate. As the anonymous saying goes, "We may not have it all together, but together we have it all." Our Army adventure lasted twenty-plus years, taking us across America to invent homes in Missouri, North Carolina, Washington, Kentucky, California, Washington (again), Kansas, Georgia, DC/Virginia, Italy, and back to Missouri to retire. How did my family survive this journey? By being intentional and grounding each day in faith and prayer, loving each other deeply, and cherishing quality family time. Life and love are about intentionality in how you show up for people, every single day.

Intentional About Raising Team Wilkins

The finest and most important career role I have ever held is that of being a mother. In the bucket list of achievements, this one is at the top. The responsibilities are immense, endless, and joyfully rewarding. As mothers, we shape much of our children's lives socially, physical, emotionally, and academically. I value all these areas and have placed a high priority on educational opportunities. It is one of the greatest gifts we give as parents to our children, aside from love. As an Army family, we were always on the go, moving every two to three years. Our children attended eight to ten schools along the way. Our faith grounded and encouraged us during these challenging transitions. Philippians 4:13, "I can do all things through Christ who gives me strength," gave all of us the unstoppable courage to go after our goals. Academic success came with structure and processes creating an environment where habits were encouraged. Routines were imperative for peak performance and to reach each child's full potential.

During this challenging time, I launched TEAM (Together Everyone Accomplishes More) Wilkins Academy to reduce gaps in our children's education. I created the *7 Life Principles Leading to Academic Success* and curated a curriculum to keep educational goals a priority, regardless of where we lived. The Academy resembled a traveling school with experiential learning. At each new assignment, we visited all the historical sights, museums, and monuments, touring national treasures such as the White House. Abroad, I wore my International Business hat and planned several excursions. We sent postcards from Italy, France, Germany, Switzerland, Liechtenstein, Austria, Spain, Slovenia, and Croatia. There was always a beautiful lesson to be learned from these opportunities: hearing new languages, counting foreign currency, sampling a variety of extraordinary foods, meeting diverse people, and admiring architecture and art. In the classroom, processes, habits, routines, structure, dedication, and discipline became the cornerstones of scholastic success and allowed Team Wilkins to reach their academic goals in high school and beyond.

Intentional About Education & Lifelong Learning

I believe that education is at the forefront of all our opportunities, and our minds are our greatest asset. It is a space where we can explore our gifts, find truths, seek answers, and grow in confidence. Our education is something no one can take away from us. Once we have earned it, it is ours to keep and cherish.

My love and passion for learning and education led me to begin my master's degree program in Education from the University of North Carolina, but the Army had different plans. I put that goal on hold for twenty years, and once we returned to St. Louis, my husband and I decided to get our masters together. The Executive MBA program at Washington University–Saint Louis was the picture-perfect fit, featuring leadership, entrepreneurialism, and global residency programs. Success happens when we continue to move forward, visualizing the goal and never giving up.

Intentionally Believe in the Power of Your Goals

For TEAM Wilkins, GOAL stands for Go Out And Live! My younger self was doing just that when I courageously headed to preschool. Being intentional is a mindset and a form of self-leadership. It is about asking yourself "What are my goals for the day?" There is a beginning, middle, and end to everything we do, and success happens when we continue to move forward. Intention is about placing tiny steps and processes in place and following through with due diligence and foresight. It requires dedication and unyielding determination. It requires patience, and thinking of several iterations to find one that prevails. It requires spending quality time with family, friends, and colleagues who are whispering truths in your life to help you "dent the world."

Through daily, weekly, and yearly repetition, small winnings start to accrue. When living intentionally, there are choices that need to be made, sacrifices that come, and no guarantees that your "intentions" will triumph. Yet if you faithfully stick to your processes, stay agile, and remain in the game with a growth mindset, you will prevail. Own your grit, have a positive mental attitude, and believe in the power of YOU! Your future is yours; create your best life and live with intention. *What are your goals for the day?*

Rachel Rubin Wilkins has twenty-five years of demonstrated success and impact as a global community leader. She brings passion, commitment, and novel solutions to build partnerships and events that enhance diverse communities. She founded Team Wilkins Academy and Team of Seven Consulting.

Rachel earned her Executive MBA from Washington University–St. Louis. She recruited for the University of Missouri–Columbia and Olin Business School. She curated marketing strategies for a late-stage technology startup that grew from $13.8 to $32.5 million in enterprise value.

Rachel's accolades include the Shield of Sparta and the Dr. Mary E. Walker Award conferred to military spouses for demonstrating unwavering, exemplary volunteerism.

Rachel serves on various boards in the St. Louis Region: John Burroughs Parents Council, SIUE CMIS Advisory, Medallion Adventure Club, Folds of Honor, and WASHU's Women's Society.

Rachel adores her family, and together they enjoy seeking adventures in the outdoors. She loves to run and has completed the Marine Corp Marathon, STL GO! ½ Marathon, three Army Ten Milers, and Shaw Bloom10k.

Natalie Goeckeler

I Pfeiffered It!

Mine is a story of the phoenix rising from the ashes. While I might spend my time here ranting and venting about my painful past, I'll choose to let you read between the lines. The journey to get where I am today has been hard fought, and if sharing my story helps one person to gather courage, focus on their strength, and find their inner and outer voice, then I count that as a win.

I've always been the gal who is the consummate fighter—to a fault. This served me well, especially when my life fell apart in one fell swoop. I wasn't the only one who was shocked. On the outside, everyone I knew was blown away that I wasn't off in a padded room somewhere. I cannot tell you how many times I've heard how it's impossible to tell if I'm struggling, upset, hurting, etc. I'm going to pull the "that's how I was raised" card. Does this resonate? I have incredible, entrepreneurial parents who instilled that fighting spirit in me, and maybe that touch of humor helped more than I realized. My mom insists she's a closet comedian, which is always good for a laugh.

While I've figured out that "unique" is not exactly how I'd describe my life to this point, I have determined what is unique is the fact that I had the courage to open up. And because I opened up, I've had several women come to me to share their personal journeys.

So here is my story. After twenty-three years of marriage to a man who had been in my life since I was twelve years old, and three beautiful children, living the only life I'd ever known, with all its hopes, dreams— BAM. Divorced. Big ouch. That's the "in a nutshell" version, and now you can read between the lines. Here is where my intention begins.

Four years ago, I was waitressing during the day while my youngest was in school. This allowed me to be her personal taxi (things have not changed in that arena) and be present for her. My career has always been in sales of some sort, but during this time in my life, I needed to be available to her as my now ex-husband traveled for work 90 percent of the time.

You know how animals can sense a storm is coming—like every single cow lying down in a pasture? Well, we humans call this intuition. It's a super strange feeling, and the cow thing is extremely bizarre (file that away for a trivia night . . . you're welcome). Changes were on the horizon. I had no idea what kind of changes or how things would play out, but I could feel that a door was opening, and I needed to walk through.

I walked through that door, and that act ultimately changed the trajectory of my life. With little mojo left in my tank, I decided to do something unheard of and taboo. I decided to focus on me. That's right, I made a conscious decision to be selfish (cue the gasping crowd). With that intuition thing floating around, I could sense a major storm on my horizon, and that consummate fighter emerged. In that moment, I knew I needed to get back to my digs in the corporate world—back into sales.

I mentioned during this time that I didn't have a lot of mojo left in my tank, so this was when I made a choice to change the internal dialogue running through my head. I told myself things like, "You're not good enough. You don't have a college degree. They are going to laugh you out of the room." I decided, instead of focusing my energy on this negativity and beginning to believe it, to do something virtually impossible—I ignored it all. Instead, I wrote down affirmations and hung them around my home, reading them multiple times a day. Even Oprah would be proud at the fact that I'd started to be intentional about daily gratitude.

After revamping my resumé and accepting an interview for the one and only job I applied to (pretty gutsy, or maybe the intuition thing again), the nerves kicked in and the inner dialogue came creeping back. I did my homework about the company, went over mock questions in the mirror, changed outfits at least ten times, and worked on stamping down the negative talk. It's amazing how much strength comes out of nowhere when you feel backed into a corner. I channeled my inner Michelle Pfeiffer, from her movie *Up Close and Personal*, and how her character basically faked her way into getting hired as a small market news anchor, which ultimately led to her becoming a major network star. It was "fake it 'til you make it" time for me.

I repeated all the positive affirmations I could think of as I drove myself to the interview, which would make anyone puke if they overheard. It's easy to second-guess yourself on the regular when you are everyone else's cheerleader, including your own. I've always thought of myself as a confident person, raised to be independent and face seemingly insurmountable challenges head-on. Years of putting my needs on the back burner and never hearing the crowd cheering for me, well, I can tell you wholeheartedly that this absolutely rocked my confidence.

While my accomplishments continued not being celebrated and, dare I say, resented, I gathered all my strength and became the person I knew was hiding deep down. It felt so strange, like I was doing something wrong. Why is it wrong to be successful and strive to be your best self? Pay attention—it is not! When people make you feel this way, you are on to something, but it's not what you think. They are intimidated by your energy.

Back to the interview. With all the self-talk, affirmations, and being my own personal cheerleader, I Pheiffered it. (Coining a new phrase, possibly?) In that moment, I became the person I knew was in there all along. I mustered up everything I could to make sure the "me" that had been stifled for so long was present. I found my voice, and that fighting spirit returned. That day was an awakening of sorts. I accepted the one and only interview I applied for, the position that more than 800 people sought, the job I knew would be mine became mine because I set my intention. I walked through that door and never looked back.

I sold myself and asked for the position. I was extremely intentional about the fight. Already being backed into a corner in my personal life, I was going to climb out of this no matter what or how silent the crowd around me. The position was ultimately offered to me, and I accepted and have gone on to manage the Midwest for a global company, closing million-dollar deals.

I made a choice that day to take my life back, to stop sitting on the sidelines cheering for everyone else's accomplishments. This was my time, my life, and my moment to start living for me and not everyone else. As that door opened and my confidence returned, I became very aware of my circumstances and made sure to find gratitude in all that was happening around me, to me, and for me. The change was miraculous.

Since grabbing ahold of this opportunity, I have deliberately shifted my focus on stamping out negative forces, which has resulted in many more doors opening that have turned my life 180 degrees for the better. I've learned throughout this process that there will always be naysayers and negative energy, but now I choose not to listen. I have realized that these folks are intimidated, and boy oh boy does misery love company. I chose peace, and this has allowed me to realize my inner strength. The journey to get where I am today has been nothing short of amazing.

While the changes in the last four years of my life have been enough to make me crazy when I truly reflect on them, I can't help but sit in awe at times. I never wanted to have to be strong. I never wanted to have to fight so hard. It's so easy to get caught up in focusing your energy on everyone else and their goals, so much so you don't realize yours are virtually disappearing.

Take the time to set personal goals, step outside of your comfort zone, give yourself permission to focus on you. If you want something, go after it with authority. All of this has led me to be a huge fan of carpe diem. I no longer turn my back on opportunities and a good fight. My eyes and ears are always open and in tune with possibilities. Bad things will happen, but I no longer choose to stay in those moments for very long. I use those moments as tools to manifest the next opportunity on my horizon.

Being intentional changed my life. Removing the fear of taking a chance and walking through that door with intention will be the greatest gift you can give yourself.

Natalie Goeckeler was born into an entrepreneurial family; her dad built a St. Louis industry-leading telecommunications company. Working for his corporation while she was in school, he made sure Natalie worked in all aspects of the company to have a well-rounded view of the business world.

Natalie owned a construction industry business for many years and belonged to numerous professional organizations. This led to her current role, managing the Midwest region for a flood mitigation company, where she travels to twelve states educating folks on emergency protocol.

Natalie is committed to helping women grow and come into their own while experiencing life-changing events. Her husband, Shawn Goeckeler, and their five beautiful children have one very feisty Boston Terrier. Shawn is also an entrepreneur, as President of Creative Supply Chain Solutions. He has been incredibly supportive, including being a title sponsor for this project. When they aren't running the "Mom and Dad Taxi," they travel and play golf.

Kristene Rosser

KMA, I'm Doing It Anyway

I was your typical small-town girl. Not popular or bombshell gorgeous. I was that girl who really didn't fit in anywhere. I was in the top 20 percent of the class. Straight-A student. Graduated with honors. Never got into real trouble. Played all the sports. Did all the afterschool activities like dance, gymnastics, etc. Started working at a local restaurant at the age of sixteen after babysitting at twelve. Summers were filled with my family driving me all over to play softball. Apparently, I was a halfway decent pitcher there for a while. I never had much time to just be a kid, because I was always studying or working. It was great.

A self-proclaimed tomboy, I was a proper small-town girl following the path I was supposed/expected to follow. I was a feisty little girl, though. I was told "no" a lot. No wasn't the word that was used all the time, but the intention was "No." I didn't like the rules I was expected to follow, or that I was to act in a certain way. Be quiet. Sit still. It was exhausting.

As I got older, I felt judged all the time. "You're smarter than that." "You're better than that." "Why are you so adamant about doing this?" "This won't look good." "Girls aren't supposed to act that way or do those things." "Stop dancing and turn that crap down."

This whole "no" thing could have gone two different ways. I could have complied and gone along with the norm. I'd squash my dreams and play the role I was supposed to play as the small-town girl who was seen and not heard. Somewhere inside, I decided that wasn't going to be the case. I wasn't backing down this time. I wasn't going to be told what to do because it's what I should be doing. I was going to color outside the lines, and no one was going to stop me. I lashed out. I dug in. I did what I was going to do regardless of all the noise. I didn't know the word *intention*, but that is what I set for myself.

Kiss my ass, I am starting the girls' powerlifting team.

I am not sure where the drive came from. I don't know if it was because I was just fed up with being told no or if I was so enamored with the sport. My sophomore year in high school, the girls' volleyball team was tasked with volunteering to work at the boys' powerlifting meet. As a member of the Junior Varsity (JV) squad, I was responsible for assisting with a scoreboard. I was taken aback by the whole scene. Watching these boys prepare for each lift. Their faces, their demeanor, their intensity. It was something I had never seen before. Each lifter went through their own pre-lift routine. Each lifter succeeded or failed. Each lifter had to be mentally and physically tough. The only job was to lift weights. That's it. Just pick up the weight. This went on all day long. It was the coolest sport I had ever witnessed.

My junior year I became *the* girls' powerlifting team —party of one.

The athletic director told me no until I threw the rule book in his face and reminded him there was no rule against it. Then my family told me no because it would be hard, and people would be mean. My classmates told me no by accusing me of being an attention whore or a lesbian (that was rude back in 1994). Then I was told no by some of my teammates (the boys who were already on the team). But I still did it. I showed up after school every day and completed all the practices. I went to every meet, even if I wasn't lifting. My coach told me he didn't have the budget for my powerlifting meets, so I paid for them out of my own pocket. No one was going to stand in my way. I didn't care if I was good or not, proper or not, I was doing it!

Powerlifting appealed to me because it was a sport where you play against yourself and no one else. It is a mental game. One that I had never played before. If you don't pick up the weight, you have no one else to blame. I had always played team sports such as basketball, softball, and volleyball, where you had to rely on others to do their part to win the game. I had never done anything like this before in my life. I thought it was the coolest sport ever invented!

Just pick up the weight. That was the job. The mind game you play with yourself to do such a simple task. To me, powerlifting embodies the word *intention*.

There was a small group of guys on the team who secretly kept track of me. I had no clue. They played hardball by teasing me and calling me names. Then, when no one was looking, they helped me through a hard lift or spotted me so I wouldn't get hurt. I knew I was accepted when one of these guys teased me and I teased back. The weight room went silent, then he put me in a headlock, pretended to punch me in the side, gave me a noogie (rubbing his fist on my head to mess up my hair) and said, "Alright, Rosser, back to work." I was in! After practice, I made it home to my driveway then broke down in tears of joy. I had defeated "no"!

I spent that first year on the team getting used to the workouts and the coach trying to get me to quit. At my second meet, he said, "If you don't bring home hardware, we aren't doing this anymore." Challenge accepted. I set my intention and brought home a first-place trophy in my weight class.

My senior year, my high school held its first girls' meet. That was cool, in and of itself, plus I won the Outstanding Lifter Trophy. Later that season, I took second place at Nationals in the 148-pound weight class behind a girl from Arkansas who broke two world records that day. I'll take second to that! Two of my secret helpers were with me that day. They took third place and fourth place in their weight classes. My heart glows with this memory. One of my helpers is no longer with us, and the other is an extremely successful businessman in Dallas with a beautiful family.

Today, my high school has a very strong girls' powerlifting team. Last time I saw them in action, there were fifteen girls participating. That made my heart shine.

Who knew my intention way back then would open the door for so many young women to experience the game of "you against yourself." What a powerful lesson to learn at such a young age. It's always you against yourself. Every day you wake up, it's you against yourself. You choose every morning if you are going to accept no or if you are going to say Kiss My Ass, here we go.

When I am not laser-focused on what I want to achieve, all things in my life come to a screeching halt. All the "healths" go crashing down. Mental health. Physical health. Social health. All of them. Then I look up two years later and wonder what in the hell happened? Oh yeah…I am living my life without intention.

Staying focused is difficult without an accountability partner. I will admit that. I find that I am better at being intentional if I have someone watching me or relying on me to be the best I can be. Without this, I simply slip back into my little cocoon and watch the world go by. It's nice and cozy there. No one bothers me. I get to do absolutely nothing if I want. It is a breath of fresh air. You know how I know I have been in the hole too long? My clothes don't fit anymore!

My intention was to overcome no, and I ended up with so much more.

To me, intention means putting all your self-doubt, negative self-talk, and everyone else's opinions in a soundproof drawer with a strong lock, and then losing the key. Once you make up your mind and you are ready to defeat yourself at the "I'm gonna lose" game, that is the intention. The act of pulling yourself up and creating your path the way you want it—that is the intention. So the next time you hear that little voice in your head telling you no or you aren't good enough or this is going to make you look bad, it's your job to scream back, "Kiss My Ass, I am going to win the game, and no one is stopping me!" and just pick up the weight and lift.

Kristene Rosser is the Owner of KRS Realty, LLC and a Partner of Tax-pertise, LLP. She earned her BSA and MSA from Southern Illinois University–Edwardsville and spent four years as a US Army Civilian auditing the US Army. Two of those years were served in Iraq under Operation Iraqi Freedom and Operation New Dawn. April 2018, she launched KRS Realty, LLC as the Designated Managing Broker/Owner with a mission of keeping real estate simple. Kristene helped found Taxpertise, LLP in 2012 to support individuals and companies through their annual income tax journeys. Over the last eighteen years, she has volunteered as a Boy Scout Leader. During that time, Kristene trained numerous Scouts and Scouters in leadership principles by serving on Wood Badge, Kodiak, and NYLT staff. She helped more than twenty young men and one young woman earn the rank of Eagle Scout.

Jennifer Church

Dream Big

I have struggled with writing this chapter. It began with my intention for my daughter, to mold her into a wonderful tiny human and guide her into being a happy, fulfilled, and successful adult. Then, while writing this, I realized that the intention of making my daughter into a successful, happy, and fulfilled adult was not about her. It was about me, and the things I did in order to show her, teach her, and instill in her that all things are possible.

Perhaps every parent can understand these intentions we hold for our children, and how they are a part of every facet of ourselves. With my daughter, these were my intentions, and my ability to provide for her well-being, her understanding, and her fulfillment. She could only become what I showed her, what I taught her, and what I allowed her to see and experience by observing how her mother lived a life guided by intention.

To make that happen, I took a step back to understand what that meant. I had to realize that an intention is not necessarily a goal. It is more than that. An intention is making a commitment to what you want to happen through your actions, your words, and your thoughts. It is the aim or the purpose in which you act or think and the energy you put forth in the things you do. These things are guided by your intention. That sounds confusing, so let's look at it in a different way. For example, if your goal is to lose weight, you don't just wake up and say, "I'm going to lose twenty-five pounds" and hope that it happens. To achieve this goal, you must actively have a plan, a mindset, and determine the specific actions you will take. Your intentions might be: I will eat better so I can lose weight; I will make sure I get plenty of sleep so my body is rested; I will commit to thirty minutes of exercise each day; I will learn about caloric intake. Intentions include a complete mindset, aligning your thoughts and actions in order to succeed.

To live with intention means, to me, that I am consciously setting a discipline for myself. We decide our intention by picturing what we want and what we want that to look like. Where my daughter was concerned, I wanted her to be a happy, successful, and fulfilled adult. To achieve that, I set my intentions on giving her a happy, successful, and fulfilled childhood, starting from the day she was born until the present day.

Morgan, my beautiful daughter, is now twenty-five years old and is exactly that: a happy, successful adult who works daily at her fulfillment in life. Honestly, as her mother, a single mother with a completely absent father, I'd give myself a grade of fair to medium. I was successful at a great many things I did, but there were others that I failed at, some miserably. I always tried, though, with the best of intentions. I wanted Morgan to understand that the sky is the limit, that she could do anything or be anyone she wanted to be. All of us can dream; we just need the imagination to dream it and the confidence to go get it. One of my successes was dreaming big.

Every night when she was little, during our bedtime routine, we would read a story, play flashlight shadow puppets, sing, or do something together. As I turned off her light, I would say, "Goodnight, I love you the most, and dream big, little girl." This was a mindset I held and an action I took to bring my intention into being for her. I wanted her to deeply know that the world was hers for the taking, and to dream big. Do anything you want, little girl, and be anyone you want to be. Dream it, live it!

I laid it out for her about how your dream becomes reality. You must work at it. You can't just wish it. Do the research, set your intention, plan, and commit to do it. Reevaluate and tweak your plan when necessary. Although there were many things I did throughout her life to teach and show her all the different lessons that parents give their children, I was consistent with this message: dream big. Every night, when she would say she'd like to be a princess or when she'd voice her other hopes for when she got older, I always replied, "Dream big, Morgan, you can do anything you put your mind and energy to." In her high school yearbook, the last thing I wrote on her Senior page was: Continue to DREAM BIG, forever. I bought her a plaque with these words for her new house, and it hangs where she can see it every day. It's one of the many things that I know has been a part of her happiness, fulfillment, and success in her life so far— the knowledge that if she can dream about it, create it in her mind, and see it, she will do it with the full support of her family and her friends. Morgan knows anything is possible if she puts her mind to it.

She has stayed true to her dream of becoming a nurse, graduating with a Bachelor of Science in Nursing. She wanted to work with children, so she went after that, and with huge success as she has a job in the neonatal intensive care unit. She wanted to move out and be on her own, so she bought a condominium. She made this investment for herself rather than paying rent on an apartment and fulfilling for someone else's dream of wealth. One of her many intentions is to be physically fit, so she has created a plan for that: she watches her diet; she meal preps so she's ready to eat at work; she's a total gym rat and goes to the gym. Every. Single. Day. She has made her intention, devised her plan, is consistent with her commitment, and has been quite successful. She has come into adulthood with a bang! Morgan is on the right track, and I could not be more proud of her. She has many dreams, and it will be truly fascinating to watch her bring those to life through setting her intentions.

It is one of the true accomplishments parents feel: watching their child, their baby, become an adult and put into play the things that were so very important to teach them. Ironically, it seems to come full circle. My mom always told me, "Can't never could." I know that I could do anything because my mother instilled that belief in me, as I did with Morgan. Several times in my life, I have had a mountain in front of me, but I knew I could figure out how to conquer it. My intention and the belief in myself led me over the mountain every time.

Intention is a way to lead your life, to not just accept the life that is in front of you each day. Take it by the hand and lead it to the things you want—your vision, your dreams. Intentions allow you to take control of your life so it can be everything you want it to be. The power of intention intertwines with the laws of attraction. You attract what you believe. Whether you realize it or not, your life will become a mirror image of your thoughts, words, and actions, as these are your intentions. If there is something in your life that you are unhappy with, assess it and find the root of it. Most likely, it's because of your mindset. I challenge you to picture your perfect life. How different does this look from the life you are living? If you truly want change and you want to live your perfect life, then set your intention to obtain this and you will manifest yourself right into it. Remember, the energy of your intention will help determine your life. Intention is always the guiding principle. Unfortunately, most people do not think of their intention; they just think of *what* they want to do, not *why* they want to do it. Consider your intention and the action plan you'll take to achieve your goal. Make the commitment to set an intention about what you want to happen. Every day, review your goal and the intentions that you have set up to achieve this. One day you will realize that you have made it your reality.

Dream big! You can do anything you set your mind to do!

Jennifer currently resides in St. Louis, Missouri, where she was born and raised. Morgan, her daughter, is her greatest love. She is in the role of Strategic Account Manager with United Rentals, a Fortune 500 company that she has called home for more than twenty years. She is a Past President of The American Subcontractors Association Midwest Council. She currently sits on the National Board of Directors for the American Subcontractors and is an internationally bestselling author multiple times. Her favorite hobbies include being with family and friends, golfing, boating, and art.

Danielle Tabers

My Superhero Mindset

"Remember that your thoughts are the primary cause of everything."
-Rhonda Byrnes, The Secret

One year for Christmas, my mother gave me a book, *The Secret* by Rhonda Byrnes. The book is about positive thinking, mindfulness, and the idea that our thoughts become things and our perceptions shape our reality. I thought, "Great, just what I need, another self-help book to collect dust on my shelf." But the book got me hooked on personal growth like it was a Netflix series. I started nerding out on podcasts and blogs, devouring any content I could find on the subject. Equipped with mindfulness, gratitude, and intention as my trusty sidekicks, I've become a superhero in my own life, empowered to master my thoughts and emotions and manifest a reality that fills me with love and respect.

Through the practices taught in the book and other resources, I learned to define my own version of success. I now understand that to grow and succeed, I must get out of my cozy little bubble of old habits, mindset, and perceived limitations. So, I set an intention to get out of my comfort zone. YIKES! I did things that scared me—like signing up for a respiratory therapy program while raising two young children, solo, even though math literally gives me hives. (Apparently, I enjoy living life on the edge.) I worked hard, excelled in the program, and graduated with honors. A few years into this career, I pushed past my fear of public speaking and took on a teaching position for a new respiratory therapy program. I became an ordained minister to perform weddings, where I had one shot to get it right and make a couple's day unforgettable. (No pressure, right?) Despite initially doubting my qualifications, I took a chance and applied for a position traveling around the country to train doctors on medical devices. I landed the job and thrived in the role. And this…this right here…this chapter you are reading, was terrifying! So terrifying, in fact, I almost didn't do it. That nagging not-so-little voice in my head was screaming at me, "Who do you think you are? No one wants to hear what you have to say! Don't make your past struggles public. That's humiliating!" I have named this inner critic of mine Gertrude.

Gertrude is an anti-hero from a childhood story passed down through generations of my family, meant to teach children the value of appreciating what you have, including difficult relationships. Her message is: Stop whining and learn to get along with your annoying little brother or you may end up an axe-murdering orphan. A nightmare of a story, to be sure, but one that imparted strangely frightening, yet valuable, life lessons, such as developing an attitude of gratitude and the hidden potential for growth in difficult interpersonal relationships. Anyway, I told old negative-spewing Gertie to shut the hell up and used my well-honed superhero powers of mindful intention to kick her out of my head. Through these experiences, I learned that taking risks and challenging myself leads to growth and success. It has been said that you can't give what you don't own, so I want to share all I have learned about the awesome power of intention with anyone who might benefit from my story. This is my ultimate idea of a superhero: Having the courage to face your own demons and turning those negative experiences into beautiful flowers of personal growth. This is my superhero intention in life!

Throughout my life, I've faced many challenges that seemed impossible to overcome. During my childhood, we moved between multiple states, and I attended fourteen schools between the ages of five and thirteen. As domestic violence survivors, my family sometimes sought refuge in shelters. I never felt at home anywhere. Always the new kid, I was often bullied by other students. These experiences devastated my self-esteem and self-efficacy, and I dropped out of high school and college several times. Looking back, I realize now that the largest and scariest obstacle I had to overcome was myself.

Confronting the parts of ourselves that hold us back is like turning on your camera and discovering it's in selfie mode—a jarring experience that makes you want to throw your phone at the wall and then stomp on it! But, if you take a deep breath and keep looking, you may see things from a new perspective. Who knows, you may even capture some of your best angles along the way.

At the lowest points in my life, I felt like a complete failure and that my past mistakes sealed my fate. Imposter Syndrome was my constant companion, but eventually I realized I was in control of my own narrative. I set my intentional focus on my strengths, like my adaptability and empathy, and reframed my past experiences as opportunities to learn and grow. One of the key concepts that helped me was recognizing the importance of humor. Let's face it, when life gets tough, a good laugh can open us to a broader, more objective perspective.

Success isn't just about hitting milestones; it's about aligning your life with what truly matters to you. These are two of my top intentions: prioritize my family, and have a career that reflects my values and beliefs. I'm so grateful to have found my "work home" with Woodard Cleaning &

Restoration. Their core values are "Do What's Right, Learn Every Day, and Serve Others." The company's culture and support are phenomenal. I thrive on being out and about, building relationships with people, and engaging with the world. You know the saying "If Momma ain't happy..."? Well, as an Account Executive for Woodard, my happiness levels are off the chart! Being happy in my professional life positively impacts my family's happiness too.

To stay focused on my intentions and goals, I set clear boundaries and make time management a top priority. This includes scheduling essential tasks, delegating responsibilities when possible, and being intentional about how I spend my time. I also practice gratitude and mindfulness, which help me stay grounded and present in the moment. But let's be honest: I'm far from perfect at this! Sometimes it feels like my mind has a mind of its own. The struggle is real to balance work, family, and personal growth! Mindfulness and self-awareness help me see when I'm overdoing it and not being present in the moment. Currently, I'm spending a lot of time networking, which is fun but exhausting. Every day, I'm learning new ways to balance everything. Setting boundaries is an ongoing process, but I'm committed to it for my well-being and the well-being of those I love.

Thanks to my superhero mindset, I've conquered the workplace and strengthened my personal life and relationships. My trusty sidekicks— intention, mindfulness, and gratitude—have helped me be of service to others and to instill that same value in my children. Now, instead of just binge-watching Netflix, my family and I spend quality time volunteering at a local food bank. This activity gives us a sense of fulfillment and purpose, and it teaches my kids the importance of giving back and the joy of making a difference. Who knew that being a superhero could be so fulfilling and heartwarming? Move over, Iron Man; there's a new hero in town.

Adopting a growth mindset has been a game-changer. By recognizing that challenges and failures are opportunities for growth and learning, I have achieved success in my personal and professional life. By pushing myself out of my comfort zone, I've built my confidence and learned to embrace the journey rather than focus on the destination. If you'd like to apply these superhero principles in your life, start by reframing your mindset and approaching challenges with a positive and open perspective. Seek opportunities for growth and learning, and don't be afraid to take risks and try new things. Taking care of yourself and prioritizing your well-being will enable you to be your best self and achieve your full potential. Remember that success isn't just about reaching your goals; it's the twists and turns, the challenges and victories, that make the journey worthwhile.

In addition to mindfulness, gratitude, and living with intention, I've also learned the importance of seeking support from others. My friends, family, and mentors provided me with the emotional support and guidance to overcome my self-doubt and achieve my goals. So, build your support system and surround yourself with positive and encouraging people who will help you stay motivated and accountable. Seeking help is not a sign of weakness, but is rather a strength, and it can make all the difference in achieving success. I'm deeply grateful to my mother, whose strength, wisdom, and humor in the darkest moments inspired me to embrace these essential concepts in my life. Now, I strive to be that same support system for others, paying it forward and helping others overcome their obstacles. Ultimately, that seemingly impractical Christmas gift from my mother opened the door to a new way of thinking and living that has transformed my life, proving that intention, mindfulness, and positive thinking are not just buzzwords but powerful tools that can help us become the superheroes of our own story.

Danielle Tabers is a dedicated and enthusiastic account executive at Woodard Cleaning and Restoration, where she works closely with commercial facilities to provide top-notch cleaning and emergency restoration services. With over a decade of experience as a respiratory therapist, Danielle brings a unique perspective and unwavering commitment to helping others to her current role. In addition to her work at Woodard, Danielle serves on the Executive Committee for FOSPA, the Facility Operators and Service Providers Association, and is an active member of both CREW (Commercial Real Estate Women) and IFMA (International Facility Management Association). Her dedication to networking and meeting new people is matched only by her love for her family, including her amazingly supportive husband, three wonderful children, and two beloved Aussie pups, Daphne Luna and Penny Lane. When she's not working or spending time with loved ones, Danielle can often be found practicing yoga, reading, or exploring new adventures.

Dr. Tiffany E. Slater

Intentionally Faithful

I started my career in Human Resources during the last year of my undergraduate program, leading me to a dream job. I am fortunate to have worked in several different industries (recruiting agency, manufacturing, property management, retail, casino/entertainment, and public education) throughout my career. Each position presented new challenges and opportunities for my professional growth and development. I met every quirky assignment and life-altering encounter (terminations and other stomach-turning conversations) with optimism and warmth. My professional success, relationship-building skills, calm demeanor, and positive outlook took me to the C-suite.

Like the chess pieces in the series *The Queen's Gambit*, I could see my next career move in my head. I knew what was next because I could envision it and it felt natural, normal, and destined. I studied my next move like I was studying for a test. I researched job openings of positions I aspired to be in to understand the requirements, qualifications, and job duties. If I didn't have a qualification or experience doing a function listed in the job opening, I worked to gain experience in those areas. My career was my chess game. I was the queen, and my career was the chess board. I didn't consult God until I had an impossible decision to make. Reflecting on it, I was very intentional about being in total control of my life. My moves were intentional as they related to where I thought I wanted to be in my career.

I was finally working in the role I dreamed about, the one I'd worked hard to prepare for and obtain. I was performing work that made others say "I could never do your job." I would think in reply: "I know. Not many people can, but it's who I am." It was the answer to the question I longed to know: What's my purpose? Or so I thought.

With three active and growing boys ages eleven, nine, and eight (the oldest being my nephew), a husband who was a basketball coach and entrepreneur, and a career that required more of me than my family, my stress levels were through the roof. Then, two surgeries within two months on very different areas of my body for very different reasons caused my reality to shift.

Stress was feasting on me, and not addressing it was no longer an option. I stepped away from a position I thought would provide me with the career-long satisfaction that I desperately needed. I accepted the fact that the universe was making it difficult for me to continue to ignore the constant tug at my soul to take a chance and exercise my faith. God had spoken and called for me to do something different. But what?

Mark Batterson said, "God prepares the called." In his book *Draw the Circle: The 40-Day Prayer Challenge*, he talks about how God gives us an assignment first and then gives us what we need to carry it out. I realized that all the roles and experiences I had, and all of the chess moves I made, did not prepare me for what God had in store for me.

I remember driving to work and crying in my car before entering the building. I heard God say (as clearly as if I had earbuds in), "You are giving my power away." That was a big aha moment, and my tears dried instantly. I had been so externally focused on what someone else would do if I left, how we would pay the bills, if I would be blackballed, etc., that

I had never been courageous enough to depend on God. Perhaps it was arrogance. I was the queen on the chess board, and now I had to trust God and let the king run the board.

This time my vision was broken. It was black. I was in a mental and visual wilderness of sorts. I couldn't see my next move. All I knew was I had to go. There was no other choice to be made. It was clear to me that God was making a statement. All I could do was say "yes." My constant prayer during the journey had been, "God give me the courage to accept your will for my life. If you light the path one light at a time, I will follow. Drop those breadcrumbs for me. I trust that you know what is best for me. I trust that you will give me the desires of my heart and provide me with all I need." So many people doubted my decision and asked if I was sure about giving up this "great" career and a six-figure salary. They asked what I would do about money. What about insurance? But the right people said, "Wow that's awesome. Let me know how I can help."

Decidedly, my next step was to do work I enjoyed, spend more time with my family, control my schedule, and produce work I could be proud of.

Taking the leap of faith to say yes to God without being able to see my next move was terrifying until I completely understood the assignment. It was the first time that the chess pieces were moving but I could not see where they were going. My chess moves were no more. All I could do was play checkers, one move at a time, fully accepting that God was playing chess on my behalf. The first move I made was toward God. I said, "Yes. I will follow you. Yes, I will trust you. Yes, I relinquish my control over the board to surrender to your will." It was the first time that I said a hearty yes to God without having all the answers. Looking back, saying yes to God was also the first time I said yes to myself, with unapologetic intention!

I had been doing God's work for him. (I think I forgot that he didn't need my help.) I assumed his control over my life by playing chess with my career instead of stating what I wanted and moving out of his way, giving him full control. Now I am clear that nothing happened for me that God didn't intend to happen, but my heart's desires led the way. My moves were calculated. I don't recall asking God what my next move should be when I researched the next step in my career. God was consulted when I had an offer or two to consider. I wonder if God ever thought, "Oh, so now you want my opinion."

Since taking that leap in trusting God, my life has been peaceful. I experience joy more abundantly, and I have time to appreciate the simple things. While I still have moments when I worry about things, those moments don't last long. God continues to show me his ability to take care of me and provide what we need and want.

If I could speak to my younger self, I would say to keep God as your North Star. We can never dream bigger than God can deliver. All of the maneuvering, chess playing, and degrees obtained can never prepare us for the awesome gifts that God is ready to give us. We just need to listen, follow his lead, and be very intentional about where we place our faith. I don't know about you, but I am still a work in progress who strives to bet it all on God—daily and with intention. Saying yes to God is truly saying yes to you because he always has our best interest at heart, even when it is painful. Be intentional about where you place your faith.

Dr. Tiffany E. Slater is CEO and Senior Human Resources Consultant for HR TailorMade—the virtual Human Resource department for small businesses and nonprofit organizations with five to twenty-five employees. HR TailorMade partners with its customers to provide seamless HR expertise for their team.

Tiffany has more than twenty-five years of HR experience in a variety of industries. She earned a PhD in Organization Development and a Master's in Human Resources Management. She is an SHRM–Senior Certified Professional, John Maxwell coach, trainer and speaker, Myers–Briggs facilitator, and True Colors trainer.

Tiffany has been featured by *Huami Magazine* and, most recently, she contributed to a *WorkLife* article, "Why bosses can be too nice, and why it's bad for business." She also served on The St. Louis Small Business Task Force, in response to the economic impacts of the pandemic. In March 2022, Dr. Slater was celebrated as a Stellar Woman Business Leader by the Missouri Minority Business Development Agency.

Kim Robertson

Playing Through the Sand Traps

In golf, there are ditches of sand strategically placed along the course. They block the simplest path to the hole and test the patience and skill of the best players. But for a novice golfer like me, they are death traps. If my ball lands in a sand trap, it will take several strokes and all my patience to get it out. I haven't been above finally picking the ball up and throwing it. Not the best example of sportsmanship. The sand traps of life are much like those of golf. They try your patience, make you question every decision, set you back a few strokes, and teach you lessons about intention.

In college at the University of Missouri–Columbia, aka "Mizzou," I lived a carefree life away from home for the first time. I grew up in a small town as the daughter of an Assembly of God preacher who was also on the school board. My mom was a teacher and coach. Our family consisted of five kids who were involved in local sports and activities. I knew everyone, and everyone knew me. It was different at Mizzou. I felt free from the perceived expectations of what everyone thought I should be doing with my life. It was my chance to start fresh, figure out who I was, where I belonged, and what I wanted out of life. I was busy making new friends, getting involved in activities on campus, and partying like a rockstar. I practiced YOLO (You Only Live Once) mentality before YOLO was on-trend. Twenty-six years later, I can confidently say that

YOLO is what landed me in my first sand trap when I was barely an adult. At nineteen years of age, full of energy and dreams for my future, I got pregnant. SAND TRAP!

SAND TRAP LESSON 1: Sand traps can be humiliating. Keep your chin up, be intentional, stay focused on your goals, and adjust as life hands you the opportunity.

You might find yourself in a sand trap if you don't line up to the ball correctly or take your eyes off it before making contact. I looked at my situation and the choices I had made to land in this first sand trap of life. I realized I didn't have my life lined up right. I had taken my eyes off my goals. I was angry and terrified of what my future would look like. Though life seems impossible when you're standing in the middle of a sand trap, it is where you grow and learn. I wanted to lie down and stay hidden in that bunker, but I knew I couldn't stay stuck there.

I was now responsible for my baby's life. After stumbling through the first few weeks of motherhood, I became focused on raising an independent, intentional, and kind daughter. I was a terrified, young, single mom. I called my sister regularly, crying. Thank God for my family's support. Without them, I don't know how long it may have taken me to climb out of that sand trap. While they would have done anything for me, I knew I needed to be responsible for my life. I was known to be quite stubborn (I like to call it independent); but here I was questioning everything and struggling with needing to rely on someone for help, and with my self-worth. I struggled to have a vision for my future, but then I would look at Ali, and my reason became clear. I now had new goals. I was determined to model skills to help build her confidence and independence.

Over the next couple years, I got married, owned a massage therapy business, went to college at night to complete my teaching degree, and had a baby boy. I was exhausted, to say the least. Ali was an early riser and would come into my room to wake me for breakfast. Sometimes I didn't get up fast enough for her. One morning, I heard furniture moving around. I went into the kitchen and found my two -and-a-half-year-old standing on top of the counter, gathering everything she needed to make a bowl of cereal. My heart dropped as I realized the danger I had allowed her to be in. My first impulse was to pull her from the countertop and tell her she could have fallen, but I quickly realized I had an opportunity to give her skills to grow. So, instead, I praised her for her problem-solving skills. Then I moved all the cereal and bowls to the bottom cabinet so she could make her own bowl of cereal on her own. On Saturday mornings I would lay in bed, listening to her making a bowl of cereal, turning on cartoons, and enjoying her morning routine. I was intentional about raising an independent daughter and showing her how to develop the tools for success.

> *SAND TRAP LESSON 2: Having the correct tools is critical. Be intentional about learning from each experience in life to build your toolbox of skills.*

My first set of golf clubs didn't have a sand wedge. I was using a 9-iron to get out of those bunkers. It didn't work very well. But now I had equipped my bag with a sand wedge. The right tool to get out of a sand trap. My husband and I had been married thirteen years when the next sand trap appeared. There had been plenty of hazards, mishits, and penalty strokes along the way. But this one was a deep bunker of sand that I saw coming. I made plans to go around it, hit over it, and I had been desperately trying to avoid it for years. We did marriage counseling, couples' Bible studies, sought advice from family, and renewed our vows. I did not want to put our kids through a divorce, but eventually it became clear that this relationship was too toxic and was no longer a healthy environment to raise them. The sand trap of divorce is deep. However, I was older and much wiser than the last sand trap. I had gained new tools, and I put them to work.

I readjusted my goals, worked on loving myself again, and started practicing daily healthy habits. I let go of people who harbored negative energy in my life and surrounded myself with healthier supporters. The divorce was most challenging for my son, Nate, who was eleven at the time. I had to be intentional about letting him grieve and doing everything I could to build him back up. I worked on myself to be able to give him that. Every day I was very intentional with a routine that included exercise, healthy eating, motivational and spiritual reading, and journaling, until it became my habit. Ten years later, my daily routines are similar. I am just as intentional with my finances. Having a deliberate plan for your day allows you to control what happens in your life rather than just reacting to what happens to you.

Happily remarried now, I am intentional in words and actions to build our relationship daily. We always kiss each other first thing in the morning, and it's the last thing we do before we go to sleep and every time we see or leave each other. I do things that bring him joy, and he does the same for me. We have tough conversations on purpose! We work on ourselves and on our commitment to each other. It is not perfect, but it is love with intention. We learned the lessons life gave us in prior relationships and added those tools to our bag.

SAND TRAP LESSON 3: Always have a plan. Be intentional about looking for sand traps and use your tools to go around them, over them, or to get yourself out of them.

When life is going well, I tend to sit back and enjoy the ride. After forty-five years on this beautiful earth, I have learned that if I sit back and enjoy for too long, one of those beastly sand traps will appear on the horizon. Though I was a classroom teacher for twenty years, it was never my dream; it was what I chose to do when I landed in that sand trap of single motherhood. After years of lesson planning—the skill of preparing for what is to come—and seeing the sand traps, adjusting the plan to achieve the same outcome has become second nature. When I was a single mom in a sand trap, I was taking desperate swings with the wrong club to try and get out. Now, I have the foresight to see the sand traps, the confidence to adjust, and the right tools in my bag to get out of them. I had major burnout as a teacher, with five years left until retirement. Seeing that sand trap ahead, I needed to make a change. But when you are five years away from collecting a pension, it would be crazy to change careers, right?

Call me crazy, because that is what I did. I didn't just quit my job and start swinging aimlessly to find another one, though. I intentionally launched my career change by creating a plan and finishing a second graduate degree. I am now the Director of Business Development at KIDaccount. We develop products so schools have the safety tools they need to protect children across the country. Great things can happen when talent and passion align.

When you find yourself standing in or in front of a sand trap of life, remember to be intentional to stay focused on your goals, learn from your experiences, and make a plan for getting to the other side. While you are there, don't forget to enjoy the game.

Kim Robertson is the Director of Business Development at KIDaccount, a school safety software company. Kim is a retired teacher and passionate about helping schools become safer places to learn. Kim attended the University of Missouri–Columbia, earned a bachelor's degree in Elementary Education from Central Methodist University, a master's degree in Curriculum and Instruction from William Woods University, and a graduate certificate in Instructional Design from Northwest Missouri State University.

At the age of twenty-one, Kim opened a massage therapy business. After twenty-five years of being a massage therapist, she enjoys helping people and considers the healing power of touch a gift from God.

Kim and her husband, Don, have three adult children: Ali, Alyssa, and Nate. They enjoy Cardinals baseball, traveling, golfing, scuba diving, and snow skiing. Kim is an adrenaline junkie. Some of her top adrenaline rush experiences include night scuba diving with the manta rays in Hawaii and skydiving.

Amanda Bohnert

Seeking to Engage, Elevate & Lead

Intention is a simple word and a simple concept. One must act with purpose and conviction. Yet it can be pretty challenging to achieve in practice. It requires forethought and passion to do or achieve something with intention. We might not even realize it, but when we act with intention each and every day to achieve our goals, we can live our lives to the fullest.

My career journey began with undergraduate degrees in public relations and management. Unsure of where my path would lead, and with a Type A personality, I knew I enjoyed planning, creating, and writing. Upon graduation, the next step on my path was to get a job. I had little expectation for that first position, nor did I look at it as a step to a career, but merely a way to pay my bills, maintain health insurance, and build my resume. Even though I always pictured myself at an ad agency, I took a position as a marketing assistant at S. M. Wilson, a St. Louis–based construction management firm. Little did I know, this position would lead to not only immense personal growth but also the ability to grow my industry by being intentional with both my words and actions.

When I accepted the position at S. M. Wilson, I knew nothing of the built environment or construction industry. Learning quickly, I found this amazing industry beautifies spaces, creates community, and transforms lives daily by building spaces where people live, work, heal, learn, and play.

I fell in love with the concept of being a tiny piece of making my community better and loved the pride I felt each time I saw one of our projects.

Through GRIT, I was able to create my own career ladder, working my way up to Chief Marketing Officer and becoming one of the six executive leaders of my firm. It was not an easy climb, but it was made easier by great mentors, a business culture of success and growth, and pure determination.

Yet being a woman in construction can be a difficult journey regardless of your role or position. The construction industry is historically male-dominated and, unfortunately, can provide challenges to career development, such as stereotyping and antiquated human resources policies and practices.

One of my greatest passions and inspirations is helping to achieve equity. Equity comes in many forms, and our world needs it to thrive. Having worked nearly twenty years in construction, I am motivated by equity for women in the workplace and within their work/life balance.

In 2021, during a lunch with Denise Hasty, Vice President of Advocacy with the Associated General Contractors of Missouri (AGCMO), she asked me over chips and salsa if I believed there would be value in starting a women's group within the AGCMO. Denise and I are long-time industry friends, having both entered the construction industry around the same time. AGCMO has groups for young leaders, human resources, safety and diversity, equity and inclusion professionals (among others), but nothing dedicated to the female professionals in our industry and region. To say I was excited and motivated by the idea of an AGCMO group dedicated to women in construction, no matter their role, was an understatement.

Within a couple of months, Denise, Charlyce Ruth with the AGCMO, and Katey Twehous of Twehous Excavating and I had our first planning meeting to create and launch a new women's group, which we had named Women of STEEL. Our first goal was to create our intention when establishing our new group. What mission would drive our success? Who was our audience? What did we want to accomplish?

Women make up just 10.9 percent of the construction workforce but are growing exponentially. In construction, women hold a variety of positions, from trade workers to human resources, project management, accounting, office management, marketing, and entry level to C-suite. While recognizing that women often have different personalities and circumstances than their male counterparts, this organization is intended to lift each other up, motivate, and provide resources for networking and career advancement. However, knowing where to start and how to launch a state-wide group seemed overwhelming. Denise, Charlyce, Katey, and I all have very different paths and life experiences. To truly understand our audience and our intention, we reflected from within, sharing some of our own experiences.

When acting with intention, inner reflection is often a great starting point. Asking yourself the why, how, and what of any action or message often provides a framework for action and response.

While sitting around a large conference table in Jefferson City, Missouri, the stories began to flow. There were stories of adversity, success, partnership, and failure. I shared how difficult it is to balance and harmonize work and be the mother of two school-aged children and how I can suffer from overwhelming guilt.

From the moment my daughter was born, the self-inflicted "mom guilt" began. How could I love this little person so much yet still want to work? At one point, a male coworker even asked if he should help hire my replacement because surely I would not want to work and be a mother.

Time is the one thing there is never enough of, and you cannot manufacture more. It is hard. Guilt that you are home. Guilt that you are at work. The never-ending hours of pre-planning and the mental balancing act game. Do you lie awake at night mentally organizing your list and plotting your driving routes to be as efficient as possible, yet still worry you will not live up to the expectation of achieving it all? Questions like these are the ones we wanted our group to answer, or at the very least provide a safe place for listening.

When Denise, Charlyce, Katey, and I shared our experiences and the stories of our individual challenges in the industry that propelled each of us to be who we are today, our intention for our women's group became quite clear. Themes had materialized. As women (and mothers), we often do not give ourselves enough grace, adding pressure for perfection. Since we are unable manufacture more time, we can support each other with time management, life hacks, and work-life harmony. Women also tend to shoulder the burden. Our new organization would create a village of support, encouragement, and resources.

We founded Women of STEEL—Seeking To Engage, Elevate, and Lead. It is open to all women in the AGCMO, regardless of title or position. Our mission statement is quite clear of our intentions: "Women of STEEL is designed to provide engagement opportunities to women working within AGCMO member firms and offer opportunities for leadership development, personal growth and civic outreach." Women of STEEL launched in 2022. When we founded Women of STEEL and created our mission, we intended to help women in our industry expand their professional horizons, learn from others' experiences, and have an opportunity for professional development. At the same time, we saw an opportunity to elevate member engagement and provide a greater return on investment for our member companies. Our initial year exceeded our expectations with an outreach to more than five hundred women, engaging member firms throughout the state.

In February 2023, Women of STEEL hosted our first conference in Jefferson City, Missouri. With more than fifty women from across the state, it was described as "incredible," "a fantastic experience bonding with talented women within the construction industry," and "a successful weekend of personal development, networking, and fun!" In my own words, it was inspiring and simply wonderful. What we had envisioned a year and a half earlier was coming to fruition. We acted with an intention to create change, and Women of STEEL is making a difference—empowering, elevating, and leading women in construction.

Women of STEEL is just one story of intention—creating action where we saw a need. As we head into the future, I hope this is a spark for others to push the boundaries, move the needle forward, and break through the glass ceiling.

With that in mind, here are some words of advice:

- Rely on your village. You do not have to do it alone.
- No matter how much you plan, you may fail, but there is always growth in failure.
- Act with intention every day to harmonize all aspects of your life.
- Be sincere and authentic in your words and actions. People might not always remember exactly what you said, but they will remember the passion with which you spoke.
- There is always room in your life for a mentor—seek one.
- Never stop being open to learning and improving.
- If you cannot embrace something fully and show passion, reconsider your approach.
- Take time for yourself and for those you love; they are your home for when your path winds and wanders.
- Listen and evaluate with empathy; you never know the challenges others face. Remember, everyone has a story too.
- Value emotional intelligence. The best leaders rank high in reading the situations around them.

- Create a plan to achieve your goals, then reevaluate and adjust; being rigid is hardly the answer.
- Believe in yourself and be passionate about your goals; you are your best advocate.

Amanda Bohnert, CPSM, graduated from Webster University with undergraduate degrees in Public Relations and Management and her MA in Marketing & Advertising. Early in her career, Amanda was named one of the *St. Louis Business Journal*'s 30 Under 30. She earned her Certified Professional Services Marketer (CPSM) credential, setting her apart as a marketing leader. In 2022, she received Webster University's George Herbert Walker School of Business & Technology Outstanding Alumna Award.

As Chief Marketing Officer for S. M. Wilson & Co., a top construction management firm in the St. Louis region, Amanda leads a team that drives marketing and business development to secure multimillion-dollar projects. Amanda is also one of S. M. Wilson's six executive leaders.

Her career grew out of her lifelong enjoyment of learning, reading, writing, conversations, and connecting.

Amanda and her husband of nearly twenty years have two amazing school-aged children.

Becki Feldmann

Stop Wishing, Start Doing

I never had a clear path. If you were to look at my resume or LinkedIn profile and see my career progression and education, you might agree. My career has shifted from graphic design to religious studies to healthcare, then from human resources to organizational development, and everything in between. Most recently, I've moved from Human Resources (HR) technology to project management, and now financial services. As you were to view my profile, you might also see my involvement in and support of several membership and community organizations and wonder "How the heck does this all fit together?!" We will get to that.

In my early twenties, my boss said I "burned the wick at both ends." She made it sound like a bad thing, and I knew she didn't really understand me. I was interested in and involved in many things, and they all helped lead me to where I am today. You could say I still burn the wick at both ends; I am simply more intentional about what I say "yes" to. So how did I get here?

This little light of mine, I'm going to let it shine…

There are many definitions of intention. The one I like best is: purpose. Purpose gives us meaning, clarity, and direction. There's a big difference between busy and full. I choose a full life—one that is intentional and filled with meaning and purpose.

Though my career journey has been varied, I've always had a clear mission: work hard, use the gifts I have been given, make an impact, and always leave things better than how I found them. I learned this at a very young age from my parents, who worked tirelessly to serve others in the best way possible. They were also what some might call "busy," but they, too, lived life to the fullest. They intentionally chose who and what to give of themselves to make the world a better place.

My world was rocked in my eighth-grade year when my dad lost his battle with cancer. My mom, three siblings, and I had to learn to live again. We did that by continuing to make an impact on the world in our very different ways, using the gifts we were uniquely given. I was fueled by the fire of my dad's legacy and the selfless strength of my mom. Why didn't this break me? Because I had purpose, direction, and intention. At the time, my friend's mom gave me a Ralph Waldo Emerson quote: *Do not go where the path may lead, go instead where there is no path and leave a trail.*

Looking back, I did that eventually, but it required determination, intentionality, and self-awareness. While I was achieving success, in ways I thought were true to my purpose, I realized that maybe I had been doing it all wrong. One of my favorite human beings on the planet, a former leader and mentor of mine, gave me a bookmark with this quote when he retired: *"Don't ask yourself what the world needs. Ask yourself what makes you come alive and go do that."* —Reverend Howard Thurman.

At first glance, you might think this quote sounds selfish (I know I did!). But the more you read into it, this quote is about intentionally living into your gifts to serve the world in the best way you can. When you do something you love, you end up having more to give.

I took on many roles over the years because I was good at them, and because when people asked me to do more and more, I did—even when it got the best of me. Nothing is ever worth that! So I reevaluated what I wanted out of life, what I stood for, who I wanted to be for my family, and how I wanted to make my mark on the world.

As I was reevaluating my career path, I was challenged in my family life too. After my husband and I had two beautifully wild boys, we decided we had room in our home and hearts for more children. In 2018, we suffered three miscarriages three years in a row. I lived in a daze for a good amount of time after those losses. I was going through the motions of everyday life, just trying to survive, but I didn't have a lot to give. I wasn't living into my purpose, and that tore me apart. I was only a half version of myself, at best.

A few things got me out of my fog: my family, my faith, and my friends. I was reminded that "Not all storms come to disrupt your life, some come to clear your path." —Paulo Coelho. Storms are often a metaphor for trauma in life. They are messy, and they displace things. But after a storm, we can see them as an opportunity instead of a tragedy and figure out how to rebuild. Though my light had dimmed, I reconnected with my purpose, which gave me the will to survive and thrive. I realized I was burned out (and taken advantage of, which was partially my own fault) at my former employer of more than sixteen years. So I flipped the script and started to intentionally rebuild the life I wanted to live, the full life I wanted (and missed).

To live my true purpose, I founded my own LLC b-e-connected, offering brand management services to help others tell their story and I started selling jewelry for jBloom. Their mission is to "wear and share your story," and this completely aligned with my values. Initially, I sold it to fund in vitro fertilization (IVF) treatments, but then it became part of who I am and what I stand for. My husband and I eventually determined that IVF would not be the path for us, so we now use the additional money for experiences with our family and donating to causes that are important to us.

Serendipitously, I came across my current role at Commerce Bank, and, again, it completely aligns with my values. My decision to join the bank was solidified when my now-boss sent an email with the subject line, "If you want to build something, this is your place." This promise turned out to be true. This is a place where people get to know you, value your bright ideas (and make them even better!), help you focus on what matters most, and they understand that this varies for each person.

Most recently, I founded a women's boutique called Lilac Ivy Boutique with the mission to empower women and build confidence through style. We promote body positivity through personal styling and shopping. We also give back through shopping fundraisers. Again, this role is aligned with my values.

Are you seeing a theme here?

Yes, I might still be burning the wick at both ends, but now it is with even more focused intention. You've probably heard the phrase: If it's not a "Hell yes!" then it's a "Hell no!" That saying was a helpful tool for a while, but I found a better way to make decisions: be more intentional about what I say yes to in order to fully live the life intended for me.

Through all the challenges, I got clear on my values: Faith. Family. Community. Relationships. Health. If I really had to bottle all these up into one value, it would be Making a Difference. A friend once said, "Decisions are easy when your values are clear." Ask yourself—Is it going to bring me closer to living the life I am meant to live?

I also have an accountability partner in my husband, who checks with me sometimes to ensure that I am aligned and living my values (and maybe, most importantly, taking time to relax!). And when I am not, he knows me well enough to send me out for a long run so I can clear my head (what was I thinking?!) and get back on track. Always have someone looking out for you to make sure you are carrying your light!

I know I am intentionally living into my gifts and aligned with my values when I see some of these things in my life come together. I am not sure why, but I am always wowed when this happens, and I thank God for all that I have been given and am able to give in return.

Do I have it all figured out? Absolutely not. But I know the values that will intentionally guide and light my way. And now you know a little about me (maybe that I love quotes!) and that I have a whole lot of living, loving, and learning left to do. And if it is your intention, I want you to live a full life too!

Join me—get clear on your values and stop wishing, start doing!

When I stand before God at the end of my life, I would hope that I would not have a single bit of talent left, and could say, "I used everything you gave me." —Erma Bombeck.

In her role as Assistant Vice President, and Senior Employee Experience Designer for Commerce Bank, Becki Feldmann provides dynamic and engaging leadership in the attraction and retention of employees. She was recruited for her energy, enthusiasm, and passion for creating great places for people to work. She puts this into action working with team members and stakeholders across the bank with a focus on ensuring employees have the resources and relationships they need to succeed, the opportunity for their voice to be heard, and that, most importantly, they feel they belong.

Outside of Commerce, Becki is involved with local HR organizations and nonprofits, co-owns Lilac Ivy Boutique, is a designer with jBloom, and she owns a brand management company, b-e-connected, llc.

Becki is a mom to two hilarious and handsome boys, who get it from her husband of fifteen years. They live a very full life and take any opportunity they can to have fun and make a positive impact in the world.

Sally Drake

Iron Intention

My story begins when I began to reach out of my comfort zone and live a bigger life. I made the decision to do an Ironman triathlon.

I grew up in a wonderful house with my mom, dad, and my twin brother. It was party central for our high school friends, always kids coming and going, and the weekends were full of festivities! My lifestyle was fun and relaxing, and my parents' only request in school was for us to come out with C's. I majored in fashion design. It sounded glamorous and promising. Fast forward to Sally at age thirty. I finally completed my degree by going to night classes while working full time in retail (not as a buyer!). I did not miss a beat and continued with school to earn my MBA. I found health. I taught spinning classes, ran marathons, and around this time a friend dared me to dabble in triathlons. Between the ages of thirty-one and forty-five, I completed thirteen full Ironman triathlons and multiple endurance events including several half Ironman triathlons, marathons, and a 50k run. I also worked as a staff accountant, project accountant, and eventually a senior financial analyst. I loved math and accounting. I felt comfortable with the regular paycheck and the ability to sock money away in my savings accounts.

Then a big turning point in my life came when, at the age of forty-five, I left my corporate accounting job to start my own business. A person who I respected suggested the idea that we open a triathlon shop together. The idea lit me up, and the next day we started the business plan. It was realistic at the time, as I had no kids and not a lot of debt to hold me back. And so it was, Swim Bike Run opened on May 25, 2011.

I was happy, on cloud nine, and feeling free and untethered as I did not have to go to the office every day and stagnate while watching the clock and doing a job that I was not passionate about.

Fast-forward to 2015. I avoided vendor calls and prayed for more bike sales. I focused on what was going well, my coaching business! I was scared but hopeful and positive that business would turn around somehow. Eventually my business coach suggested that I recruit some investors. I contacted four people who I coached in the past and were involved in the shop. I presented the budget and financials. They all pitched in an investment. Swim Bike Run would go on!

In January of 2016, I made the decision that would change my life forever. The feeling was like when I would register for an Ironman triathlon. My stomach ached with excitement knowing that the days ahead would be full of adventure and challenge! I decided to leave Swim Bike Run and start Sally Drake Endurance Coaching, LLC. This was not an easy decision. My intention from day one of writing my business plan was to succeed. The missing piece was intentional planning. Although I had the vision for this magnificent, one-stop, multi-sport shop, the reality was that I did not sit down and dig into the "how" of success. I had a forecast, a retail coach, a business accountability group, and hope—lots of hope.

Less than a year after my parting from Swim Bike Run, I quadrupled my income in my coaching business. It was booming! For the first time in my life, I reached a six-figure salary.

My business adventures are comparable to the challenges of an Ironman triathlon. The starting line was when I said "yes" to the shop and formed my business plan. The swim portion was the setup: choosing vendors, hiring resources, and building my team of employees. In the race, the swim was hard for me as I fought choppy waters, elbows, and fear— like starting this business with many questions on whether I was doing things right. The bike portion is like the years in business, making decisions along the way, managing fueling, staying strong during the darkest of times. The way I managed the bike portion could dictate how the run would go. And when I got off the bike, I hoped my depleted legs would carry me through the run portion of the triathlon. I always finished. I always ran that marathon to the end no matter how horrible I felt. Like the end of my Swim Bike Run business ownership, I pushed through in a mental marathon until I parted ways. The threshold of the Swim Bike Run side door was my finish line!

And then, a new starting line presented itself. When I least expected it, the most profoundly life-changing opportunity dropped right into my lap. While visiting my brother in Seattle in mid-December of 2019, my favorite race director in the St. Louis area called me, a man I loved dearly. He asked, "If I gave you everything you need to put on the St. Louis Triathlon, would you do it?" I slept on it and decided to dive in and accept his offer. And he did just as he said; he gave me the money, the website, the mailing list, the trailer, and equipment . . . everything! I did not know how I would do it. My days were full and exhausting. But somehow I managed to make it work beautifully. I hired an amazing, hard-working, dedicated crew of contracted employees and eventually a part-time employee. And then things took a turn in 2020 when the pandemic hit. We pivoted (there is that overused word!) and put on virtual races. People needed goals to work toward, so this was the answer. It allowed me to dip my toes into race directing and planning and to absorb as much as I could while outdoor group activities and racing were on hold in the world.

My intention with taking on MSE (Multi-Sport Experience) Racing was to keep this race director's wonderful events alive. They were valuable to the triathlon community, and I did not want to lose them. I had no idea what I was getting into but was up for the adventure!

This quote from Mel Robbins often pops into my head: "You are one decision away from a completely different life." When I decided to put on the St. Louis Triathlon, I had no idea what was ahead. I was scared and unsure, but I could not say no to this challenge. And this has been my life. Dreams that I don't even know I have come true. This is the result of my intention to fill my days with productive work, play in the sport of triathlon, and grow by taking on the opportunities that are gifted to me.

Ironman triathlons helped me dig deep, learn about myself and my ability to set goals and achieve them, and to make decisions with intention and put in the work every step of the way with the glorious, rewarding finish line at the end. All while surrounded by overachieving, supportive, and strong people.

It does not have to be an Ironman triathlon that changes a path, but a goal that allows you to grow and expand. A goal so large that you wonder if it is even possible. When I signed up for my first triathlon, which was a sprint distance (300-yard swim, 10-mile bike, and 3-mile run), I had no idea what to expect.

I just heard this in a podcast: "Ninety-four percent of all women in C-level positions were athletes in the past." If this statistic is anywhere close to accurate, this means something. When a woman faces a fear and learns to push through, to remain positive, and to surround herself with similar high-achieving gals, she grows, and it carries over into other areas of life.

When I was a kid, my parents would see me running around the yard with my long, skinny legs and call me "crazy legs." It still stings to think about it. I laughed and accepted that I was not athletic, but gangly and clumsy. This stuck with me, and I believe that deep down, it may be part what drove me to do one Ironman triathlon after another until I found a bigger, scarier goal and until people respected me as an athlete. My intention was not in the front of my mind; I was just having fun. But the accomplishments felt so incredibly good, and crossing that finish line is indescribably magnificent. I loved the feeling and the respect I gained from others. Maybe that is the respect or recognition I missed out on as a kid! A kid who would not even think about trying a sport because she was too uncoordinated and clumsy.

My wish is that I could reach out to all the girls and women who lack the confidence to reach for the stars, to those who were told they can't do more. We can accomplish amazing things, and it starts with just one goal, one finish line that will fill you to the brim with excitement and confidence that will carry on into all areas of life. Then, continue to reach beyond that comfort zone, do things that scare you and light you on fire in business and personal life, every single day.

Sally Drake, MBA, is the owner and Race Director of MSE Racing and puts on quality endurance events including triathlons and running races in the Greater St. Louis area and Illinois. She also enjoys coaching triathletes of all levels from newbie to elite, with a passion for helping them achieve or exceed their goals. She specializes in ultra-endurance, much through her experience in completing thirteen full Ironman triathlons.

An enthusiastic entrepreneur, Sally is active in her local Chamber of Commerce and a member of Inner Circle, an invitation-only women's business mastermind group. She participates in and runs sessions in Fuel to Fire, a business owner's accountability group. Sally is also a new member of the PWA, Professional Women's Alliance.

Sally's latest projects include a Women's Adventure Retreat series (the first one is open for registration) and a 501(c)(3) to provide resources and bicycles for those who cannot participate in endurance sports due to the costs involved.

Nikki MacDonald

A Woman's Touch

Women are emotional. Women are dramatic. Women are chatty. Women are distracted. Therefore, women are weak. These are common notions that we have all heard throughout our lives. Women are often compared to men and deemed less than, many times because of the above characteristics. I navigated the better part of my career believing those were weaknesses. I cringed when I saw women playing into these stereotypes and would think to myself, "You're just proving them right." For many years, I believed those were flaws that I would never overcome.

It took several personal and professional relationships and encounters for me to realize that these characteristics do not have to be weaknesses. As a manager, I have come to see these traits as badges of honor. These qualities have the power to build a fiercely loyal, purpose-driven team. Those are the teams that make lasting and profound change, and who share a mission and values that drive them daily.

Let's examine each of these "weaknesses" and intentionally reframe them as the leadership strengths they are:

Women are emotional. Yes, women have the strength to possess and express an array of emotions. We can express gratitude, joy, disappointment, fear, excitement, anger, empathy, and pride. And when we wear our heart on our sleeve, we can instill that same ability within our team. When you want a team rowing in the same direction, working toward the same mission and acting with purpose, how else do you expect to get there? *Intentionally Reframe: Emotional=Relatable.*

Women are dramatic. "Dramatic" is an adjective used to undermine passion. Women *are* passionate, driven, hard-working humans. We express ourselves and our beliefs with passion in the form of many emotions. We see strength in intentionally showing our passions and rallying a team around them. Never apologize for showing passion! *Intentionally Reframe: Dramatic=Passionate.*

Women are chatty. We talk, we express ourselves, we communicate. One of the most common complaints among employees across all industries is a lack of communication. Teams want to be informed and help to work toward a goal or solution, but oftentimes feel they are not aware due to a lack of communication. Maybe others would do well to take a cue from women and chat with their teams! *Intentionally Reframe: Chatty=Informative.*

Women are distracted. Yes, we are distracted. We take on more than most men in the name of closing the gap. We are empathetic, nurturing caregivers by nature. We strive to do it all. We added academia and the workforce to our plates and displaced nothing else. Most job postings list the skill of multitasking as a coveted trait. A woman multitasks on a level that may be incomprehensible to others. *Intentionally Reframe: Distracted=Versatile.*

Women are weak. After reading the qualities above, I hope you can see how wrong and profoundly narrow this stereotype is. Women are not weak. We take on an enormous physical and mental load, day in and day out. In the workplace, we often feel as though we are expected to prioritize work over all else and are weak if we do not. That perception is largely driven by men who are only able to make their work a priority because of a strong woman behind the scenes. *Intentionally Reframe: Weak=Dynamic.*

I implore you to intentionally reframe these qualities as characteristics of a strong leader. Instead of being a stoic leader who drives processes and efficiencies, try applying some of these qualities and watch your team rally around you with purpose and loyalty.

On my way to intentionally embracing my feminine qualities as strengths, there have been many turning points in my life and career. I started in an entry-level position and worked my way through the ranks to controller, while along the way obtaining my accounting degree and starting a family. I heard and accepted the above phrases regularly. In 2020, I left my company of twelve years after I heard the phrase, "You'll never be the successor." I decided at that moment that I would never again apologize for being a woman. I knew I could use my strengths as a woman to create a skill set that was far more rare and therefore valuable.

In my next role, I stumbled at first. I was defensive and fiercely adamant about keeping work and my personal life completely separate and balanced. Two weeks into this new job, I found out I was finally pregnant again. Two weeks later, the pandemic shut everything down. For that first year, I failed to build any meaningful professional relationships. I managed no one, and I knew nothing about anyone on the team with me. After I returned from maternity leave, I realized there was a vacuum to be filled. I remembered what I told myself in my previous job, and I set my intention to turn my supposed weaknesses into my defining characteristics of leadership.

I immediately began mapping out an organizational chart, job descriptions, career advancement matrices, processes, goals, and action plans. I built the infrastructure for what I thought a successful accounting department should look like. Then I went to work on getting buy-in.

I needed to convince executive leadership to support this idea, and I needed to rally my team around the big changes I was proposing. This was not going to happen by chance. It took extreme intention and careful attention to detail. I was very purposeful about my approach to my team. I showed them my passion for the path, but I also wore my heart on my sleeve and showed them my fears. I wanted to inspire confidence in my plan, but not come off as a know-it-all. This was a risk, but I was determined to see it through. I strategically sought support from other leaders who had experience with this structure. I was able to sell the new position to A-players as an exciting new skill set to achieve. Once I had a team of diverse and supportive members, buy-in was soon to follow.

In implementing the plan, the team has methodically set goals, created action plans to support them, and supported each other without fail as we progressed forward. I fiercely defend my team, and I tell them when they make that difficult. I understand setbacks, but I always redirect forward. I am candid about my feelings, but unapologetic about my expectations. I will be as loyal to you as I hope you will be to the team. I will feverishly drive accountability and be there to put my arm around you when you struggle. I care deeply about everyone individually, and as a team. I once thought I couldn't do that and maintain a work/life balance. I see now that it's necessary to feel purpose in your work. And when you have purpose in your work, you will naturally find balance in your life.

I believe that leading with emotion, accessibility, and relatability has made me a manager who people want to work with. I believe that because I was managed by a strong woman who led that way, and I know how much of an impact it made on me. I will not fail my colleagues, and I will not abandon them. I make mistakes, and I candidly discuss them with my team. There is no discussion or project that I lead without 100 percent intention on authenticity. I've made myself a rare commodity to any organization by making a woman's touch my best skill set.

We work in an ever-changing world. These next generations expect different and want better. Women have a place in this social shift. These innate strengths that we possess can be powerful if we embrace them and intentionally use them to usher in a new workplace. I challenge you to shift the narrative. Be transparent and open in your leadership. Empower others to do the same. Do it now, and do it with the intention it deserves. If you do, our daughters may never have to know what it was like to have to dim their shine for someone else.

Nikki MacDonald is a controller with fifteen-plus years of accounting experience in the construction industry. She is a thoughtful and collaborative leader and is responsible for the timely and accurate financial reporting of a $500M construction contractor. As a manager, leader, mother, wife, student, and friend, Nikki finds joy and balance in her life by nurturing all those relationships with intention. She and her family are St. Louis City SC Founders and love to frequent and support many local small businesses. She serves several charitable organizations in the St. Louis area through KeeleyCares, and is passionate about empowering women in leadership.

Shalia Ford

I Choose Me

"In the long run, we shape our lives, and we shape ourselves. The process never ends till we die. And the choices we make are ultimately our own responsibility." —Eleanor Roosevelt

Summer of '88

Although it's been over three decades, I vividly remember moments from that day like it was yesterday. I was sixteen. It was a warm Saturday afternoon, and I wore light blue Guess jean shorts, a white V-neck t-shirt, and a pair of white Ked sneakers. That day, I made the most courageous decision I would ever make: I chose me.

I was sexually abused as a child. I kept this deep, dark secret for eight years while the abuse went unnoticed. Those who were supposed to love and protect me did not. I kept silent out of fear. Fear for what would happen if I broke the silence and exposed the secret. Fear for what would happen to my loved ones. Fear for what others may think of me. Fear of being blamed for what happened to me. Fear of being removed from family and being alone in the world. Fear of never being loved or lovable. Fear muted my voice. I suffered in silence, and I masked my internal pain and suffering. No one knew.

When I finally broke the silence to stop living in fear, I told the one person who I came to trust and felt would accept me: my high school boyfriend. I was at home that day. With a heart full of courage and conviction, I called and told him my secret and ended the abuse. He was at a friend's house nearby and walked over to see me. By the time he arrived, the police were on the scene. There was chaos and confusion in my family, and it became clear that I would still have to take matters into my own hands. I chose to leave. That afternoon, I walked away from my family with just the clothes on my back. I had nothing and nowhere to go.

Intention is the plan or purpose behind an action or decision. It is a mental state that represents a commitment to carrying out a specific course of action. That summer afternoon, my clear intention was to be free, move on with life, and never look back. I chose me.

Education—My Way of Escape

Since I was a little girl, I have loved learning. In preschool, I absorbed all that the teachers had planned for our class, and while the other students napped, I stayed up and wanted to learn more. In elementary school, I quickly finished my assignments and asked for extra-credit work. When the abuse started at home, school became my place of escape. I felt safe there. Not only could I be normal like the other kids, but, more importantly, I was in control of the situation. Every day, I put on my happy face and left for school, choosing to excel by doing my best. This approach made me feel good about myself. I intended to get good grades, and I was a star student, earning A's and B's. Around fourth or fifth grade, I joined more school activities and played volleyball, basketball, softball, and even floor hockey. I felt safe at all the practices and games with my teammates, and it kept me intentionally away from home. In middle school, I began to dream about going away to college to escape my home life. I chose to pour myself even deeper into my academics and athletics, striving for perfection.

What did perfection mean to me? It meant doing and saying the right things. It meant wearing the right clothes and projecting an image of confidence no matter how I felt on the inside. I had to prove I was good, lovable, and worthy. The accolades from teachers and other trusted adults felt good. I became addicted to performance-based affirmation. Over-achieving, being perfect, and people-pleasing became my three-pronged strategy to shield me from the abuse I was experiencing at home. This survival tactic served me well for many years—until it didn't.

The façade of having it all together was heavy. One day while walking in a crowded hallway between classes in high school, a thought hit me: overachieving, being perfect, and pleasing people was exhausting! I decided I no longer wanted to wear that mask. Removing it proved to be a challenging endeavor, and it took years of internal work to take it off and keep it off. Yet that one mental choice would manifest into my decision to choose myself, leave the abusive environment, and make a new life for myself. Today I am intentional about being my authentic self. I choose to be vulnerable with others when and where it is safe for me to do so.

Finding Sanctuary in Community

When I left home that June day in 1988, I had no plan and nowhere to stay. I found sanctuary in a community of women who offered me love, support, and a place to call home temporarily. That first night I was taken to a shelter for runaway teens. I knew instantly that it was not for me. It felt cold, was full of strangers, and I didn't feel safe. So, the first few nights I stayed with a close friend of my boyfriend's mother, who also helped me navigate my case in court. For my junior and senior years of high school, I was fortunate to stay with my best friend and her mother. After high school, I lived with a cousin and her mother.

These women, along with a select few family members and others I would meet on my journey in professional environments and church, would be an integral part of my community and give me a safe place to remove my mask, be my authentic self, and find acceptance. They modeled for me what healthy relationships looked like. I will always be grateful for the women who opened their hearts and homes to me. They helped me heal, grow, and develop into the woman I am today. In the safety and sanctuary of community, I became intentional about choosing ways to pay their goodness forward.

Paying it forward has looked different over the years, depending on the season of my life. I often opened my home to friends, family, and strangers as a gathering place for community, fellowship, and sharing our faith. Professionally, I have intentionally created safe and brave spaces for individuals to learn and grow. I have always made it a priority to do no harm and be a safe person for people—especially women and girls—to be seen, heard, and reminded of their worth.

Faith, Forgiveness, and Finding My Voice

"For I know the plans I have for you," declares the Lord, "plans to prosper you and not to harm you, plans to give you hope and a future." Jeremiah 29:11 (NIV)

This scripture is my life verse. It reminds me that God loves me, intends no harm toward me, and gives me a hopeful future. Because I grew up in an abusive home, safety and security are important to me.

My faith in Christ has been a constant for me throughout my life. My faith and deepening relationship with God sustain me, and are my source of hope, healing, and restoration. Forgiveness is an integral part of my faith practice. By the grace of God, I have forgiven those who harmed me during my childhood, but forgiveness was for me. Forgiveness released me to heal and move on. It took time and was a process, but so worth it.

Faith and forgiveness allowed me to find my voice again. I use my voice to ask for what I want and need. I also use my voice to share my testimony and encourage and advocate for others. Now, I can own my journey without shame and guilt.

Through faith, healing, and sharing my gifts with others, I continually evolve into the best version of myself. When we intentionally choose ourselves and own our healing and development, we give others permission to do the same.

Discovering My Why—Champion of Women and Girls

It was out of the most heartbreaking and challenging times of my life that my "why" was born. We must intentionally make choices that best serve us and who we want to become. I choose not to be a victim of my circumstance but instead to use the childhood trauma I experienced to uplift and encourage other women and girls. The lessons I've learned have shaped how I show up in the world, and from them I draw insight and ideas for the transformational experiences and empowerment sessions I design and curate to support others on their journeys to wholeness, healing, joy, and fulfilled living.

I am intentional in the language I use—positive and affirming. I am intentional in the environments I choose to be in—energizing and life-giving. I am intentional about the spaces I live and work in—positive, peaceful, and calm. I am intentional about the people I surround myself with and whom I choose to allow in my inner circle—accountable, caring, compassionate, and safe. I am intentional about the work I choose to engage in, ensuring alignment with my values and mission, allowing me to use my strengths, skills, and talent to serve others.

It's your time! Your past doesn't define you unless you let it. Be intentional. Choose you!

Shalia Ford is an architect and curator of transformational experiences. She leverages her gifts to inspire others to discover and pursue their unique calling by equipping individuals to lead where they live, learn, work, play, and worship. With a heart for women and girls, she creates brave spaces for authentic connection, cultivating confidence and building community.

A nonprofit leader with more than twenty years of experience, Shalia has held leadership roles with the YWCA Metro St. Louis and the NAACP national office. She currently serves as the director of leadership programs at FOCUS St. Louis.

Shalia is a lifelong learner committed to becoming the best version of herself. She holds a Master of Business Administration and a Bachelor of Arts in African American Studies.

Shalia enjoys spending time with her family and friends, reading, shoe shopping, and traveling. She resides in St. Louis County, Missouri, with her husband, the Rev. Gill Ford, and their son, Isaac.

Karen Englert

Gifts of Desperation and Grace

A significant chapter in my life story began in February 2016. I was bundled up on another cold St. Louis day and trying to look confident and professional on my first day in a new role. I had been recruited to a well-known agency and was excited to do meaningful work. This work would push me far out of my comfort zone, but I felt ready to tackle the new expectations. Being raised in a family of overachievers had served me well, but I was about to learn invaluable lessons in pushing myself too far, losing my authentic self, and putting metrics before quality.

From day one, I was hot out of the gate working statewide on policy and system changes, building allies, and creating long-term sustainable improvements in cardiovascular health. I was recognized with numerous city, state, and regional awards, including the Rookie of the Year Award for our entire eight-state region.

All outward signs pointed toward a successful, long-term career, but inside I was miserable. I was not just burning the candle at both ends; I had run out of candle.

I traveled 60 percent of the time, indulging and hiding in unhealthy extracurriculars, becoming distant from family, and compromising my ethics. Immersed in a heavily male-dominated field and fighting for my voice, I lost sight of core values that had served as guideposts. More than that, I became numb to the most integral aspects of my life. By early November 2018, I knew something had to change.

I often joke that God has a funny sense of humor, and his wit was in full effect during this period. I was helping create a healthier Missouri but killing myself in the process. Life caught up with me and handed me a few significant crises that ultimately helped push me to a new mindset, and to set new intentions for my life.

During this time, a local nonprofit contacted me about a position. Their offer was a dramatic change in career, including a pay cut, but it would mean I could stop traveling and get back to my roots in nonprofit leadership. I was uncertain, and as a person who thrives on problem-solving and thinking strategically, I was uncomfortable.

I had been given the gift of desperation, and, though afraid, I intentionally made the decision to embrace it. Living in fear is paralyzing, so I chose instead to lean into it. This meant getting brutally honest with myself, my loved ones, and my teammates. I took some time off to determine what would be best, what made sense for me, and what should come next. I reevaluated my priorities and reestablished my non-negotiables. Sometimes it is not about changing just one thing; it is about being willing to change everything, even in the face of fear and uncertainty.

I intentionally connected with my personal board of directors/inner circle (something I recommend for everyone, but especially women) to get their feedback. I prayed hard and said "yes." It was the best yes I have ever said, personally and professionally. Fast-track one year from starting in the new role, and my much improved and healthier self was tapped on the shoulder to run the organization. I intentionally repeated my same trusted decision-making process and said yes.

With this promotion to Chief Executive Officer for Boys & Girls Clubs of St. Charles County in early March 2020, I took the reins just two days prior to the pandemic lockdown. Now the real work started: I was responsible for the business, our employees, and the children and families we serve. All G.R.I.T. components were put into play, but, above all, I had to be intentional in my decision-making related to the physical and emotional safety of our team and members, along with the financial security of our business.

With support from our board of directors, I created innovative approaches to reimagining core programs and services to meet the needs of Boys & Girls Clubs of St. Charles County, both short and long-term. This period allowed me to examine many of the systems in place and determine if these were anchors dragging us down or roots that needed nourishment to further our mission. I removed a lot of anchors and focused on pouring into the essentials: our staff, our children, our families, and our community partners.

By navigating a safe reopening in June of 2020, we became the first adolescent-serving organization to resume in-person services post-lockdown. With safety as our primary concern, the return to live programming provided the means for essential workers to maintain employment, as we were able to provide full-day summer camps for member children. In addition, I set a goal to keep every single staff member employed, and not only accomplished this but also brought all the frontline staff back with a higher rate of pay.

During this time, I engaged board members, major donors, and corporate partners with the utmost transparency and professionalism to expand our base of shareholders. While these efforts initially provided a critical reprieve to weather the storm of economic instability, they ultimately have sustained a new era of development for the Clubs. By intentionally strengthening core business systems, we were able to set growth goals that were both aggressive and mission focused. This was thoughtful strategic work, and I am so proud of the results.

Coupled with the acquisition of new funding to support an increase in the fleet of transportation vehicles, an influx of financial gifts positioned us for continued growth beyond St. Charles County. In August of 2022 we opened our first school-based unit in an adjacent county and reached maximum enrollment prior to the program's launch. To continue the expansion, three Title-I schools were added to the service area to meet the growing needs of families falling below the poverty line. Of the pivotal moments in my career, this expansion, and our ability to keep all staff employed during the lockdown, rank in my Top Five.

This was intentional and meaningful work, and it was a heavy lift. I had set in motion core changes to our business model, and there were days of both clear, calm seas and massive waves with strong currents. There were times when I felt uncertain, exhausted, and scared. The things we want most are often on the other side of fear, so I had to be afraid and do it anyway. Fortunately for me, I have a solid north star always keeping me on the right path. My husband, Jeff, makes me a better human being and leader, and I am blessed beyond measure with his love, support, and guidance.

I am incredibly proud of our resilience, our commitment to our mission, and our focus on doing what we do best: creating great futures for our Club kids, families, and staff. I believe great futures not only need a foundation but rely on a lifetime investment, both of which require purposeful, thoughtful decision-making and action.

Life has taught me a lot about failure and the grace that can be discovered within it. Writer Anne Lamott once said, "I do not understand the mystery of grace—only that it meets us where we are and does not leave us where it found us." This resonates with me so deeply. At this point in my life, I am not afraid to make glorious mistakes, acknowledge and own them, and transfer the lessons to my next endeavor. I intentionally live this example daily and encourage my employees to follow suit.

While I am passionate about providing needed resources to the children we serve, I am motivated on an even deeper level to serve the greater community. I understand that no organization stands alone, independent of the effects it may have on its neighbors. I also know that no leader stands alone. I am only as successful as my team, and with the right dynamic, a unified drive, and diverse perspectives in place, everyone wins.

The last seven years have taught me many valuable skills. A dear friend shared a motto by which I try to live and work. Simply put, it is not about being right, but rather about getting it right. Living this each day is easier when I focus on my core values as a leader, our organization's mission, and the hundreds of people in my care. This means I must be intentional in acknowledging my mistakes, owning my bulldog mentality, pushing myself and others, standing firm in my non-negotiables, and extending grace. Embracing each day with this mindset makes me the passionate and purposeful leader that I am meant to be.

I encourage you to live, love, and lead with intention. Live in congruence with your deepest-held values and beliefs. Be intentional in your interactions and contributions. Lean into discomfort so you can stretch and grow. Strive for overall success, not just a specific outcome. Then go lead, achieve, and empower others along the way.

As the Chief Executive Officer, Karen works in partnership with the Board of Directors, staff, and volunteers to develop high-quality business strategies, ensure alignment of objectives to advance the mission, and oversee all operations and business activities for Boys & Girls Clubs of St. Charles County. Karen holds multiple advanced degrees in Education as well as her Certified Fundraising Executive (CFRE) designation. She is passionate about providing the resources our community's children need to equip them with a vision for their future. Karen works to unite and lift people by encouraging collaboration, exemplifying mentorship, and engaging in service.

Karen takes pride in her ability to develop strong people and teams. She has gained recognition as an influential leader and is a frequently requested speaker at local, state, and regional events. She excels in helping other nonprofit leaders develop their staff teams, improve board engagement, and create actionable strategic plans.

Suzy Barbosa-McBride

From Multicolored Flower to Me

As I was growing up, I witnessed my grandma and her outpouring of love into the community. Through her acts of care and kindness, I've learned that being intentional demands commitment. Estelita became one of the most important people in my life, shaping my identity, thoughts, intentions, and actions. To paraphrase James Redfield: "Energy flows where intention goes."

That's right! My grandma taught me how to give back to the community and create space for others to be included. She valued being a good citizen, loved her neighbors, and was a resource for them. In her simple, practical way, she was a high achiever by sheer generosity and compassion. I remember her visiting friends on weekends and helping them if they were sick or just needed someone to talk to. My grandpa, Felisberto, was a small businessman. He created jobs for the community and sacrificed his age and health to take care of our family and serve his neighbors. With these two people as my first inspiration in life, I learned how to become intentional, be present to others in need, have educational goals, maintain a positive mindset, and be a community leader.

I grew up in the northern region of Brazil, the Amazon rainforest, a place majestically exploding with nature, rivers, and exotic wildlife. This region is known by its indigenous tribes, with their legends, myths, and spiritual perspectives. Regional migration and an extensive miscegenation have made Brazilians one of the most ethnically diverse people on earth. Our country is known as "the lungs of the world," but our cultural diversity, crucial to understanding our people, may be underestimated. In my history, Brazilian-Amazonian ancestry and values were ingrained in me as I grew up in a small town, with my family, grandparents, cousins, and a predominantly Catholic community in Manacapuru, which means "multicolored flower."

I was born in this town and stayed through most of my high school years. Then I moved to Manaus, the capital of Amazonas. My paternal great grandma, Raimunda, was a descendent from Portugal. Her husband, João, was an Amazonian descendent from a river community. Members of our extended family still tease each other regarding the disparate physical traits of skin tone, eyes, and stature. My maternal grandma, Estelita, was of partly African descent; my grandpa, Felisberto, descendent of people from the northeast who made the Amazonian forest their new home generations ago.

My goals as a young adult led me to the neighboring state of Pará, city of Santarém. I experienced a cultural shock when speaking with my Amazonian accent. Kids teased me. Their accent was just as funny to me, but I was the outsider. My surprise came in discovering that I enjoyed these people, their music, their food, and their abundance of gentleness. My relationship with them shaped my skill as a communicator. It was like learning to swim early in life, with so many rivers.

Communication can come like a river to you, in waves. Sometimes smooth, but often rough enough to shock you into new awareness. Being intentional is very personal. Like waves, it can be very subtle, or not. In communicating with others, we need to recognize our origin and what distinguishes us, then embrace it as a strength, without defensiveness. We are called to our unique character, and in the process of each choice we must learn to take risks. It is the risk of being oneself! We cannot make excuses for who we are, our origin or history. We cannot expect ease, but with dialogue, respect, and commitment to mutual communication, we'll enjoy our relationships with others.

Reflecting on my experiences as a young adult, I see that my intention was toward the community. Through many roundtables and workshops, my community learned to make a difference and learned about each other's lives, roots, family histories, and values. We recognized the stereotypes each of us had and clung to for years. For three years, I was surrounded by community leaders who influenced and were in turn transformed by the community. In my vision of the community, I grew to appreciate how commitment and mutual growth go hand in hand.

In 2003, I traveled to Italy, my first time on another continent. It was a great opportunity to experience not just another country but also myself, with new awareness of my strengths, vulnerabilities, and the deeper truth underlying them. For many of us, when we are in unfamiliar space, we are deeply challenged to understand what we are not, and who our hosts are. It is useless to hide, and we are called to face ourselves. We have only to open our eyes and accept what we see, loving the image or not, and to challenge ourselves to reintegrate in various ways.

I spent six long months immersed in Italian culture, visiting amazing places. I learned with women from more than ten different cultures. This distance from Brazil challenged me to view my country more critically, its highlights and its shadow side. I confronted my own values and put them into a new perspective. I learned that culture could be influenced in many ways, positively and negatively. I had not noticed the deep level of diversity in my country until I got to know other people from different cities. One country, same language but with many accents and skin tones.

But I also confronted the prejudices and stereotypes. I felt that differences make us unique, and I liked what I saw.

On returning home, I seemed to have lost my "Amazonian" accent. My friends noticed and reacted. Was I losing my identity? Did I betray myself by the change? Not at all! On the contrary, in the encounter with another culture, I found myself. This was part of my continual call to self-knowledge, to understand who I was and my destiny. Indeed, it was a deeper journey to "self" that I never imagined—prolonged and often painful, but necessary.

I came to St. Louis, Missouri, in July of 2009 with a fiancé-visa. It was a process with many twists until becoming a reality. It was risky! I faced American laws and visa requirements, navigating between Brazilian and USA policies on immigration, and dealing with multiple and inaccessible authorities. One year into this transition, taking English courses in the International Institute and fully committed to my higher education, I made a radical rediscovery of my identity. I felt called to contribute to my Brazilian-Latino community. I became a mother while completing my associate's degree at St. Louis Community College at Meramec, then transferred to Webster University to get my bachelor's in business administration.

I used to say that St. Louis chose me, through many solid means of support, and I am honored to be here. I have found a vibrant community of leaders, and amazing friends. I continue to be transformed as a multi-cultural leader. In this community, through many partnerships, my eyes are constantly opened to intentionality. I have always been a high achiever, and it was easy for me to get involved in many activities around campus, making an impact on others like me, from distant countries. Because I was often the "go-to" person, I volunteered for many organizations, helping other students to find their voices, coordinate events, do community outreach, or simply accompany someone to get a service around campus. So, becoming intentional begins with this sense of belonging. I want to maintain a positive mindset, reach goals, and be more present, but also set a vision for myself and change it when necessary.

I am very grateful for all the paths taken and for all the people I have met already, for the many who supported me to be a better version of myself, and to all my teachers who helped to cultivate my love of education. I am grateful for my St. Louis family, and for their continuing support during all these years. Today, I am always trying to move ahead with purpose. I hope to continue opening doors for others, and collaborating with those who inspire me to spread hope wherever I go.

Reflecting on my life's intention, instilled in me by my grandma and grandpa, I now know that my personal roots and origin have been fundamental to my self-discovery, identity, and belonging. With this knowledge, I can own and assume my life. We cannot pick our ideal family, but I learned how to accept mine. I am very grateful for who I am and how I continue to grow. My personal traits are part of my ancestors, and I am so blessed with their gift of life. I feel the diversity in my veins, and the more intentional it is, the more able I am to accept it. I also accept and rejoice that I am not alone. I have my ancestry. I have my own family! I encounter new partners constantly. I am constantly called to embrace new aspects of my journey. Each of our lives' experiences are uniquely ours, so let's be proud. The journey is worthwhile! Be intentional about it!

Suzy Barbosa-McBride is from Brazil and moved to Missouri in 2009. As Business Development Coordinator in the International Institute of St. Louis, she is dedicated to supporting immigrant and refugee entrepreneurs by working with groups and community leaders to foster financial empowerment. Her passion is helping others to find their voices and to overcome challenges. A board member for the Viva Brasil Association, she has been affiliated with the organization since its foundation in 2012. As a program developer for the Brazilian Catholic Community, Suzy is a member of the Immigration Task Force of the Archdiocese of St. Louis. Currently, she is part of the Brazilian International Women's Leadership Commission, associated with the Brazilian Consulate in Chicago. Suzy holds a Bachelor of Science from Webster University and an associate's degree from St. Louis Community College at Meramec, both in business administration. With her husband, Patrick, and son, Joe, she likes to explore nature, reading, gardening, singing, and enjoying life!

Luciana Sabatino Cross

The Silver Lining

For most people, it takes until young to middle adulthood to realize their purpose in life, while for others it may take a lifetime. Fortunately, I found mine as a very young girl in the middle of a soccer field in conversation with my father, who was my coach. He said that some people may be good at certain things, while others excel in other areas. He pointed to my heart and said that while I may not be the next soccer star, I was given this incredible heart that would allow me to help others. Not many people are given such a heart, he said, and that God gave me this to make a difference in others' lives. From that point on, I knew my purpose. My intention to use this big heart would guide me and all the people I met throughout my life's journey.

Throughout my young adulthood, I excelled in my purpose of helping others by visiting nursing homes, volunteering at local homes for those who were disabled, through conversations with people needing a shoulder to cry on, and eventually in my first career as a special education teacher. The world of education had many pitfalls, however, and at times there were many barriers to my true intentions to improve these students in and outside of the classroom. I often felt stressed and discouraged. After several years, I realized my purpose and intentions were not fully useful within the classroom, so I returned to college and earned a

Bachelor of Science in Psychology. To truly realize my intention to serve students, I would need a second master's degree in the field of clinical psychology. Eventually, I was working my two dream jobs in the field of psychology: in the hospital setting during the day, and as a college instructor of psychology in the evenings.

Looking back, I see that God took me through these various routes to find my true placement and purpose. I helped hospital patients toward a better quality of life, and I shared my passion for psychology with young adults as teacher, mentor, and friend. My heart was filled with joy. Some felt that I had sacrificed my own happiness to fulfill this purpose, but I saw it another way. As my father had told me, I was given this heart to bring joy to others. In doing so, I received an immense amount of love and happiness in return. People are often described as either "givers" or "takers," and I was a giver. It was lonely at times, but in the end it was worth it.

Then suddenly, four words completely changed my life. From as far back as high school, I have always had health issues—odd symptoms that were not visible to others. Though treated by many doctors, I was not taken seriously. As often happens to women, my symptoms were ignored or minimized. Many doctors would say I was mentally ill, which was not necessarily untrue, as I did experience trauma and abuse outside the home, earlier in life. At the same time, other doctors would accuse me of being a "drug seeker." Even with a diagnosis, these accusations continue and create barriers for proper treatment. What caused the pain was invisible to them, and I did not appear to be sick. At some points, the pain and other symptoms were so unbearable I did self-medicate for lack of prescribed pain relief. One morning, my vision was growing worse, and by the evening, while teaching, I lost almost all vision in one eye. I quickly reached out to an eye specialist who had a background in neurology, and she thought it might be a case of optic neuritis. She asked about other symptoms, and I explained my experience over the previous fifteen years within our healthcare system.

Finally, for the first time in my life, someone listened and believed my story. An MRI led to a spinal tap and diagnosis. The four words that would forever change my path, purpose, and intentions were spoken to me: You have Multiple Sclerosis (MS). Rather than breaking down in tears, I sat in silence. I felt bittersweet relief knowing these symptoms were real and that now I could do something to improve my quality of life and continue my path. I know now that if I had not been living my purpose and intentions to help others, I probably would not have made it that far in life. My symptoms felt less severe when I was giving to and helping others. There were many times I wanted to give up on this life and take the easy way out, but I never did because I knew I was meant to be here for others.

Unfortunately, after the diagnosis and various medications to prevent further damage to my brain to slow down the disability's progression, I grew more ill every day. Discouraged, I was also bullied by my coworkers at the hospital, the trauma of which still affects me to this day. As one who was raised by very strong and independent women— my mother, maternal grandmother, godmother, and Aunt Earlene—I never thought other women would bully me. As a woman, I could be just as strong as anyone else. Although I did not have to share news of my health with my coworkers, I believed it was necessary. As a giver I thought this would create a support group of others surrounding me in my workplace. Instead, the constant trauma brought on a great deal of stress, until one day I looked in the mirror and did not recognize myself. I was down to one hundred pounds, and often dragged my leg or passed out at work, some days finding it hard to walk from my parking spot to the hospital shuttle.

The time had come. I would now have to be the "taker" instead of the "giver." I realized if I were to ever be able to stay true to my intentions, I needed to take a step back and allow others to take care of me. This decision led me to move home to Illinois and live with my parents. I felt so ashamed and was quite uncomfortable with all the love and support. Their care was a bit foreign to me. I also reconnected with old friends, and one who forever changed my outlook in life and showered me with unconditional love and support. This dear friend is now my husband. After a few years of getting the proper medical help, surrounded by family and friends, I was ready to relive my purpose again. I had no idea I would find this in a form of therapy, after picking up some paint and canvas at a local art store.

Being stuck at home alone every day, I became more and more lonely, depressed, and anxious. I needed to find a hobby that was not too strenuous and would provide me with some sort of relief. This desire led me to create artwork with acrylic paint on canvas. This hobby was a game changer for me.

As someone who suffers from the various symptoms of MS, chronic pain, and mental illness, I discovered how calming the painting process can be. When creating a painting, I learned to choose my colors based on my emotions. As I paint, I literally pour my emotions onto the canvas and experience a wonderful release when moving the colors around with my hands. When I gaze at the finished paintings, my emotions and tears flow. After painting for several months, I discovered that these paintings could benefit others by allowing them to find their own meaning or connection to the piece. My artwork's purpose is about relieving my pain and emotions, and it also allows others to find a sense of calm and personal meaning. Never in my life would I have thought I could find such a powerful sense of energy from a painting, and then pass it on to someone who needs such a piece in their own life.

While living the giver's life, my path has not been easy, and I'm not sure why I have had to suffer and continue to suffer. Through my journey, I have taken numerous detours, but knowing my true purpose and intentions, I have always found a way to serve others. So please know that unfortunate circumstances and times of suffering will more than likely happen; but if you stay true to yourself and your belief in what your mission is in this life, you will always find a way to continue. My only regret is that I have been unable to have a child of my own, but I take some consolation in creating through my service to others, and through my artwork. If for some reason I would die tomorrow, I hope for one thing: to leave a legacy of love. I will never be known as the woman who had a great deal of money or who achieved some high social status, but rather as a woman who accepted her true purpose and intentions at a young age, and even with all the trauma and suffering found a way to stay true to living a life to serve others.

Luciana Sabatino Cross is a newfound artist, by a chance happening, using painting as a form of therapy, due to a life-changing diagnosis. Prior to painting, Mrs. Cross completed a Bachelor of Science in Special Education, with a minor in Psychology, as well as a Master of Science in Educational Administration. To further her purpose in helping others, Luciana also earned a Bachelor of Science in Psychology and a Master of Science in Clinical Psychology, allowing her to work in the hospital setting and as an instructor of psychology at the college level.

Luciana currently resides in her hometown of Lebanon, Illinois, with her husband, Kyle, and her playful lab, Sonny. Luciana enjoys fishing with her father and her husband. In her free time, Luciana loves to create new paintings, and most of all she adores being godmother and aunt to her nephew, Luca.

Monique Block Bynum

Cleared for Takeoff

Do you remember the song "I Didn't Know My Own Strength" by the late, great Whitney Houston? In the song, she sang about crashing and tumbling and how her entire world crumbled, but she got through all that pain by finding her strength.

Her song lyrics were the epitome of an affirmation mantra of mine as I took a journey down a road that was foreign and quite intimidating. It wasn't a road—that word seems too romantic. It was more of a dusty path embedded with gravel and seeped in hot lava.

I was newly divorced. I relocated to a new city without family. No friends. No support system. But I had a job offer and an inner burning to be intentional about getting the next chapter of my life right.

I knew I had to be intentional about providing my children with a healthy co-parenting environment. I witnessed firsthand from family and friends how a non-amicable co-parenting relationship could have long-term negative effects on children. I also knew that I had to be intentional about determining what I really wanted from life, especially as I approached the age of forty. I asked myself, "What is it that you want this time?" Legitimate question. But I didn't know the answer. I had to dig deep. Like, grab the metaphorical shovel and go to work. It was kind of like the lady digging all the gunk from out of your big toe while getting a pedicure. I had to go that deep. I had to reconnect with myself. I had to figure out what I wanted, who I was, and what I stood for. I had to be proactive in creating a deep sense of intention in every aspect of my new life.

The first year was intense and filled with doubt. I was a hot mess of emotions. Although there was beauty in my new beginnings, there were also challenges and setbacks. Yet I knew that I could not succumb to adversity and despair. Instead, I used those moments to learn and grow.

Initially, as I was building and recreating my new life, I felt as though everything was a constant nagging distraction coupled with mindless quests from everyone around me. It felt like I was a participant on *American Ninja Warrior*, running from obstacle to obstacle and then falling face first just before reaching the finish line. I had to consistently remind myself to focus on purposeful living.

Choices were big for me. No longer could I make emotional, on a whim, one-sided, short-term-thinking choices that were not well considered. That's how I used to roll, but I could no longer be that or do that. I had to be intentional and committed to reframing my thought process and challenging myself to cultivate a new growth mindset.

There was so much that I needed to reprogram and rethink. I had to reclaim clarity! I didn't have it. But I knew I had to be intentional about prioritizing my expectations and the path to getting there. There were times in the middle of the night in the stillness and silence of my room where I would lay awake and repeat to myself: "respect the journey you're on." So, for those of you reading, respect the journey you're on.

As my first year of transition continued, I began to choose activities, friendships, and moments that were in direct alignment with the life I was creating. I resigned from living a life that was pleasing to everyone else except me. I bid farewell to those days. I started to do things that brought me genuine joy. I painted my life in color—no more dull, boring taupes and grays. I was the Black version of Rainbow Brite, infused with colors of happiness, joy, and peace. But somehow it began to teeter on obsession.

As I immersed myself in making progress, my behavior and attitude changed too. I genuinely thought I was building a place of intention and clarity, but things weren't becoming clearer. I was saying the words "intention and clarity" without acting on them. I was becoming obsessive about being instead of doing. I realized that there was a complete difference between being obsessive and being intentional.

I knew I was being obsessive because I was so *fixated* on change instead of becoming *clear* about change. I was so focused on getting to the end result without actually taking all the necessary steps or defining the clear goals to get me there. I wanted to be healed without going through the healing process. My extreme attachment and obsession with wanting to fix my life became unhealthy. Obsessiveness was based purely on emotions, and we all know how ill-fitting emotional attachments can be.

I was going through all the "right" motions: journaling, reading uplifting books, posting inspirational memes on social media. All good actions, but they had no legitimate substance behind them. They were obsessions. I was obsessed with getting it right. But I had to put a purposeful effort behind it. I had to do the work. I had to be intentional.

I put an immediate halt to the obsessiveness. The last six months of the first year of my transition became more challenging. This journey was difficult, but once I truly began the process of getting intentionally aligned and clear, the work I put in became a deeply intimate investment in myself.

It was beautiful, how much I learned about myself. I discovered new qualities. I discovered things that I didn't like, but thought I liked them because I was people pleasing. I found new hobbies. I became less distracted. I found love again.

As I reflect on my transformative pursuit, there are things I continue to work on. Not being a people pleaser is one of them. Staying in my lane and not focusing on the distractions around me is another. I'm always in beta mode, continuing to learn, explore, and grow.

As you think about being intentional in your life, consider the following:

- Be Burger King: That's right. Be Burger King and have it your way. Know exactly what you want and then go get it. The problem is that sometimes we have no idea what we want. This is an act of self-discovery that will likely take time. But as you know, it will be time well spent. Completing this step will allow you to have so much clarity and alignment.

- Be a Baby: Did you know that a baby's brain has upward of 1,000 trillion synapses? With this number of synapses, a baby can form so many pathways and connections that allow them to process new information. So, being a baby allows you to be in beta mode, and be intentional about continuously learning, growing, and adapting. This mode gives you room to explore new things, step out of your comfort zone, and refine your outcomes. I encourage you to be in a state of curiosity. Read, listen to engaging conversations, explore, and expand your world.

- Be Mae Jemison: She was an explorer. A seeker. She was the first Black woman astronaut to travel in space. Go out and be a seeker. Be intentional about finding and cultivating meaningful relationships. It's important to build a network of people who you want to be around—those who uplift, empower, and support you. It promotes growth for both parties. You may be surprised at how much these types of relationships can bolster your journey to being intentional.

- Be Authentic: If all else fails, just be you. Intentionally you.

Monique Block Bynum is a high-energy and vibrant professional who is also a wife, mother, author, and speaker.

Currently serving as Community Investor/Education Relations professional for The Boeing Company, Monique oversees corporate citizenship strategies that include grant and sponsorship allocations, volunteer engagement, and K–12 STEM-related outreach.

Education has played a significant role in Monique's professional journey. She holds a bachelor's degree in Communications from Rockhurst University and a master's degree in Public Administration from Syracuse University.

Beyond her professional accomplishments, Monique is deeply engaged in her community and driven by a strong commitment to disability advocacy. Monique strives to raise awareness, challenge stereotypes, and advocate for policies and practices that support accessibility and inclusivity.

Monique's love for family is evident in her personal life, as she and her husband, Mike, have a blended family of seven. Outside of work, she enjoys football, traveling, cigars, and hosting enjoyable gatherings.

Marcy Bursac

Reveal Your Heart's Intention

"Do something that scares you every day." - Eleanor Roosevelt

I climbed into bed after packing for the next day's long-anticipated and much-needed Kentucky vacation. My body was happy to collapse, but my mind had a new message for me. All I wanted to do was close my eyes and get some sleep, but my mind spoke louder: "You should go into pageantry."

"I'm sorry, you must have the wrong number," I silently replied. "I have never done a pageant in my life. Good night." I laid my head on my pillow and closed my eyes.

My mind insisted that I get up for ten minutes and fire up my laptop to research what options even existed for pageantry.

"Ugh. Fine," I conceded. "I can stay awake for ten minutes, then I want to go to sleep."

Pushing myself to crawl out from under my warm blankets to explore this wild idea led me to my heart's intention, believe it or not. I got into pageantry, was crowned United States of America's Mrs. Ohio, and then placed in the Top 16 in the national competition in Las Vegas. I earned a record-breaking 6,000 votes as the Mrs. People's Choice and was awarded a $3,000 grant for my family's foster care adoption partner, the Dave Thomas Foundation for Adoption.

Taking a leap into an arena where I had zero experience felt totally irrational at the time. Looking back, I now see that my mind was only trying to help me reveal my heart's intention: to find forever families for children just like mine.

Do you want to live with a clear purpose that results in considerable impact? Three guiding principles helped me reveal my heart's intention. Applying them can be scary but is ultimately worth it to live life with intention. I invite you to try them on so you can reveal your heart's intention too.

Thoughtfully Invite Others In

When we workshop our ideas with trusted people who are real with us, we can more clearly hear what our heart is trying to say.

My husband and I chose adoption as our Plan A. His grandfather was orphaned and never adopted, and I had served in an orphanage with older girls in Eastern Europe. After adopting our preschool-aged sibling pair, I became increasingly aware of the number of children who are still waiting to be adopted in the United States.

I had a burning desire to find ways to get others to pay attention to these overlooked children.

In the privacy of my bedroom, the idea to do a pageant was just in my head. Part of me was embarrassed, and another part was unsure what anyone else would say if they knew. As I got more information and felt a strong pull to do it, I decided it was time to invite others in.

First, I ran the idea by my husband. He encouraged me to complete the application.

Whew. He didn't think I was crazy.

Then the opportunity evolved, and I was asked to represent Ohio rather than Missouri, where I live. Someone had already been selected for my state, but no one had interviewed to represent Ohio. That sounded bogus. Certainly, that didn't make sense.

I confided in a close coworker, hoping she'd find this just as odd as I did. Instead, she told me to figure out how to make it work. I didn't want to hear that, but I agreed to survey friends and family in Ohio just to prove my point. My sister, who lives in Cleveland, thought it was a great idea. A friend who is part of a large mom blogger community in Columbus took the idea to carpool and surveyed a group of moms. An hour later, she told me they voted and decided as long as I wasn't a big fan of Michigan (their football rival) they were 100 percent behind me.

I couldn't believe that this idea might fly.

With no one rejecting the idea, I went to my final approver—the Dave Thomas Foundation for Adoption. The organization has been my family's foster care adoption partner since the beginning of my adoption journey. Surely, they would see the misguided idea.

They questioned if the pageant system knew I didn't live or work in Ohio. I confirmed they knew. They told me no one had ever asked to do this. We signed an agreement, and I began preparing for nationals.

Why was it so hard for me to hear my own heart's intention? The way my heart was leading me was nothing I had ever done before, and it didn't logically make any sense in my mind. By thoughtfully inviting others in, I was inviting them to show me what I couldn't see. In turn, I learned how to listen differently.

Learn to Listen to Your Heart

If the thought of getting to know the core of yourself feels uncomfortable, you're not alone. I would be lying if I said it doesn't come without the hard work of addressing your past, your fears, and your insecurities. So, buckle up and hang in there as you continue reading.

Months before even thinking about pageantry, I received an email asking me to invite local families to an information session about adopting children. This approach seemed short-sighted because children across the nation need families. Someone should do something about that, I thought.

Famous last words, right?

I was so angry about what I saw. It felt so wrong, like someone had muted the volume on the voices of children who were waiting to be adopted.

Sometimes our heart screams because we are supposed to be driven by anger to do something.

I grabbed a piece of lined paper and wrote down the ways someone could do something. After I filled up the page, I realized: maybe I could help. I wrote "one hour a week" at the top of the page.

Then the perfect storm happened: pandemic stimulus payments came.

My husband and I were both employed. We didn't need the money.

One night after our kids went to bed, I was in my bedroom again, sitting under my cozy blankets and thinking about how we could use that money to help others. I could write down conversations I'd had with others explaining the foster care adoption process. I printed out a blank calendar for the next month, grabbed a pencil, and mapped out how I would write a book that would walk others through the process of adopting through foster care.

Beaming with pride, I presented my plan to my husband. Within moments, I realized I'd failed to cross-check my plan with our family calendar. We had an anniversary trip planned for the very first weekend, over the three days where I'd committed to begin the writing process.

My husband asked, "Why is that a problem? I'll take you to a library each day so you can write."

I figured out what I was supposed to do next simply by giving myself a few minutes with a pencil to write out a plan. Try setting a timer for yourself for ten minutes and see if you can reveal what you're supposed to do. Try to let whatever comes to mind be a valid idea. Set no limits, even if it makes you uncomfortable. In the final principle, I will show you how to overcome that.

Embrace the Uncomfortable

Some of us avoid feeling uncomfortable.

I got a call from the pageant director. She explained there would be an interview, swimsuit, and evening gown competition. And I'd need to wear five-inch heels for the on-stage part. It was a good thing our conversation was a traditional phone call, because my face gave away my feelings of shock. I covered it by choosing my tone and words carefully.

The call ended, and I told my husband the details. He could see my shocked expression but responded logically, "So, order the shoes and start practicing."

Along with learning to walk in five-inch heels, I did several things over the next few months that took me out of my comfort zone, including getting fully naked in front of strangers to get spray tanned, getting a Brazilian wax, and making quick wardrobe changes backstage.

When I had the idea of doing a pageant, in my mind I was using the microphone and spotlight to shine light on children who were waiting to be adopted. The vision I saw did not include the uncomfortable things I'd have to do to compete. It's a good thing I was blind to the details, because I probably would have run the other way.

How did I muster through the uncomfortable? I knew my why, my intention. In fact, I wrote it down. I knew who I was doing this for and why I was doing it. That drove my perseverance through the process. It also led me to find help to realize my vision. That meant asking five friends who are counselors to be available to support me each of the five nights I'd be at nationals. It also meant crowdfunding support so I could acquire the wardrobe, travel, and hire a pageant coach. I learned to be "coachable," and I have brought that mindset into other arenas of my life.

By defining my measurement for success, declaring my ambitious ideas publicly, and aligning my time to my heart's intention, to date I have taught more than 11,555 adults to see the 113,000 children who need a forever family in the United States and how to adopt them.

When we reveal our heart's intention, our heart trusts us to use all we are to let it live out loud.

Scaling her lived experience as an adoptive mom of a sibling pair, Marcy Bursac advocates for the thousands of children in the US foster care system who are waiting to be adopted through her free app, children's book, how-do book, monthly podcast, classroom lesson, speaking engagements, and TV, radio, magazine, and podcast appearances.

Marcy is a Congressional Coalition on Adoption Institute Angels in Adoption® Honoree from Missouri with Senator Blunt and the founder of The Forgotten Adoption Option and creator of the Foster Care Adoption Awareness Reading Program.

Marcy holds master's degrees in both philanthropy and business. She and her husband live in St. Charles, Missouri, with their two brave children and three rescue canines.

Please invite Marcy to speak and connect her with those you know who have a heart to adopt and need help navigating the complexity, emotions, and/or red tape of the process.

Sabrina Westfall

Intention Is My GPS

Once upon a time, I was driving our family to Atlanta for a basketball tournament. I don't know how far we were into the drive when everyone got quiet and I started to daydream. My GPS was on but silent. I was loosely aware that we had about three hours left and twenty-seven miles until our next transition. I began to have an imaginary conversation in my head. (Hopefully someone reading this can relate to doing this thing, so I don't sound off my rocker.) I was deep in this conversation when I looked down and realized I missed the turn, and we were now four hours and seventeen minutes away from our destination. This missed turn was going to make my daughter late for her first game. I didn't say anything to my quiet family, but internally my organs grew warm, my cheeks went flush, and I started to sweat with panic and guilt. What a silly mistake I'd made because I got distracted with my own thoughts, I ignored my GPS, and turned off all my senses when I should have been on high alert.

Have you ever done this? Have you had all the tools and all the directions, but some silly distraction got you way off course? This happens in my business all the time. The to-do list, the manual, and the road map go out the window, and I react to what's at the top of my inbox instead of the priority for the day. My intention gets replaced with distraction.

In starting my business, the hardest part, hands down, was figuring out what to do each day with no direction. In some ways, I had hit the ground running. We had a few contracts and I had two employees, but I did not have a solid plan and I had very little money. Imagine sitting at a red light with your foot fully on the gas but you are in park. It was kind of like that. People were requesting things that I didn't understand. There were weeks that I forgot to write payroll checks, and don't even get me started with payroll taxes. How many can there be? I realized I needed to find some focus and define some processes if I was going to make it. I had to become intentional about everything I did.

I had the sudden scary realization that I knew nothing about starting a business. I had a lot to learn and to do. I started by writing a to-do list every night before I went to bed. I would listen to podcasts and TED Talks about business while I was at my computer learning to do data entry and balance books. I would take time out of looking at projects to read articles and books about business. If something grabbed me, I would immediately put those key tasks into place. At first it was easy things like putting everything on a calendar. I got so used to this that if it was not on my calendar, it didn't exist. I missed a few meetings early on, but this encouraged me to be even more intentional about how I managed my time. I created weekly time budgets where everything is allocated from drive time to family time. If I learned an email sales and marketing strategy from a podcast, I would immediately type up the email and put it into practice. I was starting to focus my drive and ambition with some intention, and I was reaping the rewards. My company sales more than doubled every year, and the opportunities grew from small residential projects to being a part of major historical projects including Union Station, Ballpark Village, and The St. Louis CITYPARK soccer stadium. My personal time was even more balanced between chores, paying bills, and fun family time.

Being organized and balanced is not necessarily in my nature. My grandmother is one who kept a dust-free house even though I never saw her pick up a broom. I joke that she used to make the beds before we even got up. Her finances were in order, her kids were well dressed, and she never missed a church service. However, I never knew how she did it. I saw the fruits of her labor, but I never actually learned what she was doing to keep things so together. On the other hand, my mother was more of a free spirit. Our home was less than tidy, we shopped at the thrift store, and I don't think her finance skills were very good. I am not knocking my mother. I had a fun and loving childhood with many, many great memories, but there were times that we went without electricity and heat when I was young.

My mother and grandmother are phenomenal women, and I couldn't have been better blessed. However, either I missed some important lessons from them, or I was just not wired as an organized, together type of person. I share this with you to say that it takes a lot of work for me to keep things together. One of the first things I knew was that I was not going to be successful on my own. I would have to take advantage of all the help I could get.

I encourage everyone to have a coach or a mentor. This person may change as you grow, and that is perfectly OK, but an accountability partner will help you keep your focus on your next target as you live a more intentional lifestyle. I have been working with a wonderful business coach for many years, and I owe him every credit for the path to my success. He has a great sense of humor, and we have very productive meetings, but he never goes easy on me. The first conversation I had with my business coach went something like this:

Business Coach: "Sabrina, what was your intention when you started your company?"

Sabrina: "To make lots of money!"

Business Coach: "Really? Is that all there is to it? I mean weren't you already working a decent job?"

Sabrina: "Yes, that is true. I was making OK money, but I wanted to have more control over my money and not be limited."

Business Coach: "What would having more control over your money mean to you?"

Sabrina: "It would mean we could go on more family vacations. It would mean I could buy my kids a safer car when they start driving. It would mean I could have a more comfortable retirement. I would mean I could make meaningful contributions to my community and set a good example to my children."

Business Coach: "So if I asked you again, what is your intention behind starting your own business, would you give me the same answer?"

Sabrina: "No, I would say my intentions are to live a purposeful life, to be an example to my children and other young people, to leave a legacy to my family and my community. My intention is really to change the world."

It took time and much good counsel and advice before I started taking steps to make my days better. If I had to summarize all the good advice I have gotten, it would be to take these three steps: identify your motivator(s), create an intention map, and evaluate your habits.

Using my discussion with my counselor, I identified these motivators: more time with family; retire comfortably; and contribute to my community. When I felt myself slipping back into bad habits, I would ask myself how my actions would affect my motivators.

The next step was to create my intention map. This step takes the motivators and puts an action item to it. Here is my sample list:

- Create an annual savings account for family vacations by depositing $xxx each month.

- Meet with a financial advisor quarterly to review retirement plan of having $xxx of spendable funds by age sixty.
- Create space for summer interns each year to be recruited from an urban trade program.

These action steps should be well-described, detailed action items that are time specific. If there is a dollar goal, be sure to state what the dollar amount is.

The last step is to evaluate your habits. This means that now that we have our intention map, all our processes and our habits should point us in the direction of these action items. The magic in this is that it can really identify areas where we may not be operating efficiently, or even eliminate things that are not necessary.

I will leave you with this: Do not silence your GPS. Do not get distracted by things that don't help you reach your goals. Each day should be an exciting next step toward reaching your goals, whatever they may be. Have fun in the process of mapping out your journey. Collect some great new friends who are going encourage you along the way. Learn about yourself as you clean out your proverbial cupboards. And last, give yourself a little grace. Every day may not be perfect, but if you are moving with intention, every day will bring you closer to your destination.

Sabrina Westfall is a proud St. Louis resident and graduate of St. Louis public schools. Her educational background includes an accounting and finance certificate from Webster University. She worked in accounting for a short time while starting her family as a wife and mother of three beautiful daughters. After completing her apprenticeship and continuing to work in the field, she went on to pass the exam to become a master electrician. Throughout her time in the field, she mastered her craft and deepened her understanding of the industry. Sabrina organized J. West Electric in 2014. J. West is now one of St. Louis's top emerging specialty contractors. The company has played key roles on major projects in St. Louis including Union Station, America's Center, Ballpark Village, and the new soccer stadium. Sabrina looks forward to continuing and improving her exciting journey as a business leader. Many thanks to a supportive family, amazing team, and relationships with some of the most respected influencers in the industry.

Alison Niermann

Release and Rise Up

At beginning of a yoga session, the instructor asks each person to set an intention for the practice or day. Sitting on my mat in the eucalyptus-infused space, I gently close my eyes, straighten my spine, and focus on breathing. Then I think about my intention.

I began focusing a lot on intention after my husband's heart attack. The week after a beach vacation with friends and our families, my husband woke me at 3:00 a.m., pointing to his chest and softly explaining that we needed to move fast. During the pandemic, I wasn't allowed in the emergency room (ER), so I watched the love of my life and best friend move through the sliding doors and get quickly admitted. Then I waited for the doctor to call. (Well, first, I called my dearest friend.) Within twenty minutes, the Chief ER doctor was on the other end of my phone explaining my husband was either having or had a massive heart attack, and that they would do everything they could and would try to keep me posted.

Click. Silence.

Waiting alone in the breaking dawn is surprisingly still, quiet, and daunting.

I have had a lot of scary moments in my life, but nothing prepares you for that moment—100 percent blockage of the right artery. More than a dozen doctors informed us that he might have died if we had waited just minutes longer.

My husband sets intentions every day, whether he realizes it or not. Every day, he announces that it will be a good day. He focuses on his goals and how to achieve them. Then he does. He also clears the space in his head, heart, and life for anything that fogs or could potentially block that intention.

We hear about it all the time, the power of intention. But it never really sunk in for me until I almost lost him and witnessed his approach to life.

I believe intention is a choice. It is the conscious decision to do something for a specific reason with a purpose behind the action. It's important to be fully present and aware of what's important in our life today. To clearly define and achieve an intention and be fully present, we must first release anything binding us to the past, weighing us down, and decreasing our clarity and strength to move forward. It's crucial to release everything that conflicts with your intention. This is the stuff we hold on to that fogs our thoughts and steps. It's the old pains, the nagging voices of doubt, the insecurities. We must clear it before we can climb toward our dreams.

Back on the yoga mat and through therapy, I began to release.

Inhale. Exhale. Release the hurt of being sexually assaulted in a fourth-grade classroom. Release, later being told I should have known to fight harder.

Inhale. Exhale. Being told at twelve years of age that my talents meant nothing, and my dream should end after my leading role on stage in front of a live audience of 4,000.

I repeated this over and over to release multiple pains.

I released the memory of the youth pastor who mockingly prayed over me in front of a group so I wouldn't drown in the shower due to my small frame.

I released all the times I was gaslit, unseen, silenced, and overlooked.

I released being told by someone close that graduate schools wouldn't want me, even after being highly recommended by acclaimed professors.

I released reading a text which read, "I can't believe she told me you were opening your own firm. Surely that can't be right. That's not something you can do."

I released almost losing my infant child to a heart condition.

I released living in what I call "walking in a three-year valley," including: our older daughter breaking her skull, resulting in six surgeries; my husband and younger daughter t-boned by another driver, resulting in third-degree burns and a severe concussion; a family member's mental health death; a family member's sports concussion with brain bleed concerns; four more family deaths; three school lockdowns; a toxic work environment; and my husband's heart attack.

It takes a lot of energy to carry around negative emotions and thoughts of the past and to give someone or something else so much power.

When I carried all that around, it consumed the brainpower I needed to give to my intentions. Looping the past in my mind prevented me from living fully in the present. I freed up this energy and focused on what I wanted for my life moving forward when I released past emotional pain.

When I catch myself feeling chained down to the past or focused on negativity and fear, I remind myself of when I worked on the film *Gone Girl* as a stand-in, leading to a speaking part.

I pursued it relentlessly. There was no Plan B. It never occurred to me that I might not get what I wanted. I was not focused on the voices of doubt planted in my head. My intention was clear, and I learned we must see what is possible as a reality in our minds. When we release the burdens and refuse to let them have power over our steps, we rise above it and are free to chase our purpose and dreams.

When seeking release for a clear intention, breathing goes beyond simply inhaling and exhaling. For me, it's one way God speaks to me. Looking back, I see now how his whispers led me out of the valley, back to a path to lead me to the mountain of abundance, blessing, and gratitude.

He spoke clearly to me about where to focus my daily intentions and gave me four words to remind me of the steps to take in my path: Purpose. Actions. Talents. Helping.

To define and achieve our intentions, we must focus on the following:

5. Purpose. For many, we have different purposes in our career and personal lives, and it's important to identify a purpose or desired outcome for those various aspects. Envision what you want your career to mean. What do you want your life's legacy to be, and what do you want to achieve? Reflect on your why, your interests, and what your vision statement would be for each purpose. We were all designed for a unique purpose.

6. Actions. What actions must you take each day to move closer to each purpose? It may start by retraining your mind to focus on growth and possibility. When pursuing your purpose and intention, it's easy to overload ourselves with activities that may open a door. Often, chasing everything produces nothing that moves you in the right direction. Identify the right groups and opportunities that align with your purpose. Include visualizing reaching that goal and incorporating your daily actions to reflect who you want to be.

7. Talents. Take note of all your skills and talents that were uniquely gifted to you to produce those actions and fulfill the purpose. When the voices of doubt enter your mind, refocus on what makes you unique.

8. Helping. Make space to help someone along the way.

When you release the chains of the past, it unleashes all the possibilities of the future and allows you to be fully present today. This refreshed mindset gives us the power to set our journey instead of allowing it to guide us. It frees us to set our intentions, shine a light for others, and achieve the fulfillment we all deserve.

Inhale. Exhale. Begin.

Alison Niermann, CEO of Tilley Workforce Solutions, has more than twenty years of translating business vision into people strategy, transforming recruitment, and leading workforce solutions. She started Tilley Workforce Solutions to help elevate the personal and business success of others.

In her career, Alison pioneered broadcast and employment branding through data-driven metrics. She launched global succession, intern programs, and wrote Equipped for Excellence, an interactive training guide. Today, she delivers workforce planning and executive recruitment that blends innovative AI and grassroots approaches.

Alison founded Youth Led, Inc., has media and film experience, wrote and produced a historically inspired film, and founded the area's first digital parenting publication. Alison has served the community as a mentor with Women's Unlimited, a Parent Teacher Organization Class Vice President, a St. Louis Film Works board member, and an advisory council member for TechSTL.

Alison is fueled by talent, driven by strategy, and moved to make a difference.

Ly Syin Lobster

Sobriety, Faith, and Intention

When I was in sixth grade, I felt overwhelmed. I had changed school districts after fifth grade and struggled to fit in with my peers academically. I thought I could catch up if I could have some days off. I took an overdose of my grandma Helen's prescription pills and an over-the-counter medication and washed the pills down with wine to make me sick and get me out of school. During the days off, I could pull it together. I was not suicidal then, but during high school, things changed. I started overdosing on over-the-counter medicine and binge drinking. I realized at the age of eighteen that there is no such thing as a baby alcoholic: You are either an alcoholic or not. After completing inpatient treatment at Christian Northwest Recovery Center, I relapsed. After my relapse, I thought about my future if I continued drinking, which scared me. I decided to try sobriety for real. I set an intention to survive and not allow alcohol to destroy my life. I knew that after being a suicidal teenager, I wanted to exist more than die. My last alcoholic beverage was on July 5, 1990. At the time, I didn't understand how sobriety would change my life. Now, I know how this one intention changed my life for good.

A few years into sobriety, I was despondent over my abusive marriage. My pregnancy was a pleasant surprise because I didn't think I could have children. I was concerned about the timing because I was in college.

I considered an abortion, but I realized it was my body and my choice. Even if my then-husband didn't want the baby, it was ultimately my decision. Being a single parent was scary, but I thought my child deserved better. I was the fool having a baby and believed in the expression, "God takes care of fools and babies," which gave me some courage. My intention was to try and provide my baby with a good start. My first action was to move off campus to escape my abusive spouse, and I applied myself to my college studies. My attendance improved, and my GPA increased. My daughter inspired me to leave an abusive marriage and put effort into college.

Even though I was in college, I had never thought about graduating. I had pictured my then-husband graduating and thought about how happy I would be for him, but I never imagined graduating myself. Growing up, I was repeatedly told I was dumb, stupid, and a fool, so I thought I lacked the intelligence to graduate college. In sobriety, I learned the concept of taking "one day at a time" to cope. I applied the same idea to college. I didn't focus on the future; I just focused on getting through one day at a time.

We were required to attend the Lux Series Convocations at Southwestern College, but I skipped them. I went to the Mass Communication office and typed my essays instead. This was so I could finish my homework earlier and spend time with my daughter. During my last semester, I took extra classes because I learned from Social Services that my childcare assistance would terminate at the end of the year. As a full-time student, I could not afford childcare for my daughter without childcare assistance.

I was turning in assignments until the deadline, wondering if I would pass the semester. I went to the academic dean's office the day; they were mailing notices to those who did not pass that semester. I asked him to check and see if my name was on the list. When the dean saw I was not on the list, he congratulated me and told me I'd graduated. Keeping my intention in mind, I managed to stay sober and graduate college.

In college, I didn't realize that intention and faith can enable a person to overcome obstacles. I thought I was just lucky and that is why I graduated. I didn't realize I'd earned my bachelor's degree. Five years after college, I was a single parent without stable housing. I saw desperate women at the Atlanta Day Shelter. I didn't know what would happen if I gave up hope, but I didn't want to find out. My intention while I was unhoused was not to become *hopeless*. If I allowed myself to lose my hope, I would become overwhelmed. Being unhoused was difficult, but I felt it was necessary to cling to hope to survive the experience. Despite all I had been through in sobriety, hopelessness was the one thing I avoided. After living at several shelters and house-hopping, I reluctantly returned to Missouri to live with my family.

I heard Chris Gardner's story on social media a few years later. Gardner went from an unhoused single parent to a stockbroker and finally a brokerage owner. Gardner's autobiography *The Pursuit of Happiness* inspired me. I realized that, with intention, an unhoused person could overcome obstacles and eventually become a millionaire. His identity was close to mine: Gardner is Black, and he struggled financially before experiencing homelessness. He was a single parent with no help from the absent parent. I could relate because I was a single parent without emotional or financial support. Gardner's intention was to design a better life for himself and his family. I, too, desired a better life for my family.

Also, I met a man during this time, and we got engaged and moved in together. Soon, I realized I was in another abusive relationship and grew despondent, just like when I had been married. I realized after a miscarriage that I didn't want to marry him, but I stayed with him. I thought I couldn't leave because I didn't have a job or transportation. An employment specialist refused to help me find employment since I was in a domestic violence relationship. During a checkup with my primary care physician, he told me I was so healthy that I'd live to be one hundred years old. I knew I didn't want to live emotionally miserable for that long. Staying sober at this time was a real struggle. I was afraid that the consequence of intimate partner violence would change my life forever. I changed my intention from existing to thriving. With my life coach's and others' support, I finally left my then-fiancé.

From there, I went to a domestic violence shelter where I had stayed twelve years earlier. In addition to individual therapy, I attended a six-week group therapy for women who had experienced intimate partner violence. I realized I had not healed from those abusive experiences. I used Chris Gardner's experience as inspiration to change my life. Like Gardner, I focused on my career to change my situation. I had completed my coursework and certification for being a virtual assistant before getting involved with my ex-fiancé. While in the shelter, I began marketing my virtual assistance businesses to potential clients. I secured office space and registered my LLC with the state of Missouri. In 2015, I was selected as a Top Ten Finalist for St. Louis Training and Employment Agency's Micro-Enterprise Business Plan Competition.

My decision to stay sober all those years before changed my life. I endured many hardships, and sobriety taught me about faith and intention. The coping tools I learned because of sobriety helped me deal with the traumatic experiences in my life. In 2017, I put the skills I gained as a virtual assistant to use as a legislative assistant at the Missouri House of Representatives. When I worked as a legislative assistant, it was my intention to be one of the best legislative assistants and help the state representative I worked for serve the people of his district. In 2019, I was listed in *The Missouri Times Magazine*'s 100 People to Know in Jefferson City. Currently, I am working for a nonprofit that helps strengthen neighborhoods. It's not directly related to solving homelessness, but they are focused on ensuring neighborhoods provide families with the ability to thrive.

Ly Syin Lobster is an executive assistant and mother of two adult daughters. As a second-generation St. Louisan and a formerly unhoused person, her interest in affordable housing and community development led her to Invest in STL.

Ly Syin advocates to increase awareness about the impacts of domestic violence. Ly Syin has empowered women in business, ministry, and nonprofits through Ladies of Inspiration Success. She has advocated for criminal justice reform through Exodus Reentry Village. She has volunteered with nonprofits to make a difference and improve the life quality of life for those in her community, including Ferguson 1000, which, after a successful pilot, expanded into Global 1000.

In 2019, she was listed in *The Missouri Times Magazine* in the Lifesavers category of 100 people you need to Know in Jefferson City. Ly Syin received a 2019 Transformation Award from Imagery International, a women's empowerment group founded by Enzear Layne, for her personal and professional growth being an overcomer of domestic violence and sexual abuse.

Maureen Hergenroether

Check Your Impact

We all have a million little intentions in the choices we make throughout our lives every day. Whether to be comfy for the day in sweats or look our best by dressing up. Drip coffee or needing that extra zing with espresso. The selections we make are rooted in the intent for that day and our plan for that moment in time. We are constantly acting on intentions.

But what about our bigger intentions? The bold ones? The ones that transcend our lives?

What is "intention"? It's my conscious choices that guide the plan of how I want to fulfill my purpose. It's a complex roadmap of ups and downs with no final destination, except to stay true to my desire to make a positive impact. To try and do better.

My passion and purpose is social change. I'm an equity advocate and an impact addict. My dopamine comes from seeing people's lives improve, systems fixed, and barriers broken down.

I've spent years narrowly focused on that intention, but only in recent years have I started to notice something that is paramount to intention… impact.

There was no massive life event that unveiled what my intention and passions were or should be. The discovery has been organic, though there have been plenty of moments in my upbringing that shaped my path.

I spent the first few years of my education at a Catholic school paid for by my grandparents. My dad had left, and my mom was scraping by to support my two older sisters and me. My grandparents believed it was mandatory that we get a religious education. My social status at the school was not hidden among a population of wealthy children. Old shoes and a hand-me-down coat were my attire.

One day in kindergarten, a little girl walked up to me and handed me a party favor bag. "I had a birthday party this weekend and you weren't invited. My mom didn't think you could afford a gift."

My six-year-old brain recognized what it meant to be the only one in the class not invited. It meant exclusion. It meant shame. What I didn't comprehend was the label of bias at the time. I wasn't sad, but mad. I was angry, but not in an expressive way. I was quietly angry.

I sat in quiet anger for a lot of my childhood. When I witness people being excluded, treated unjustly, or ignored, my quiet anger rises. Over the years, it's gotten louder.

As I grew older and attempted to step in, fix things, save things, and try to improve, I found the outcomes could be frustrating. Ever feel like you're trying to help but just can't win?

One afternoon as a senior in college, I was driving home from class. I saw a large black dog run into a traffic crossing at a four-way stop. I felt physical pain thinking about the dog getting hit. My brain weighed the danger of pulling over and running between traffic to catch the dog versus driving off and living with the wonder and guilt of doing nothing.

As I observed no one trying to help—barely even swerving to avoid the dog— my quiet anger rushed over me.

Gritting my teeth, I quickly pulled over and started yelling for the dog. The dog ran farther from me, weaving in and out of traffic. I frantically pleaded with it to come off the road. After a few minutes, I called a nearby friend to help. As I walked to greet my arriving friend, I turned my head to keep an eye on the dog. There, at that moment, I saw an outline of a black furry blob lying in the middle of traffic. My heart sank. The dog had been hit.

This was one of the first times for me that the impact was far greater than the intention. My intention was good, but the outcome wasn't. Is it possible I made it worse? Did I scare the dog into running from me? The intent was good. It was pure. But the impact was devastating.

Impact. It's not always what you intend.

We've all said "I didn't mean for that to happen" or "that's not how I meant it." Our intention is misaligned from the impact. We're human. We make mistakes. It's not always in our control.

When you plan your goals and then build your intentions to get there, you must consider the conflicting impact that might not be right in front of you. You might not see it.

Early on in my career, I intended to work in corporate giving for Fortune 500 organizations. Companies have the power to make the biggest social change. In fact, corporate entities these days are more trusted to improve society than government, nonprofits, and NGOs.

I was thrilled when I finally had the opportunity to lead the management of a company's philanthropic investment portfolio. Leveraging my passion for big community impact with corporate budget and measurement tools was precisely my intention.

My first week on the job, I was reviewing renewal grant applications. I came across an organization serving pre-K children in severely under-resourced areas. My company had provided funding for the last five years. The measurements and impact were solid. It was a worthy community program. But I had been working in the business world for a while, so I was well versed in corporate goals and scrutiny. The program didn't align with the company's social responsibility goals. It would not help our impact model to meet our goals that public stakeholders would scrutinize. Although we had funded it for years, it had flown under the radar. If I was doing my job well, I needed to pull funding.

Without much hesitation, I called the executive director. I explained the goal misalignment from a business perspective. She was silent on the other end of the phone. I'm not good with awkward silence, so I continued to justify my case. It seemed very clear to me. It didn't fit—Philanthropy 101 in my mind. Finally, after about ten minutes, she responded, "Well, that's devastating. These are the poorest of the poor kids, and this program brings them joy and hope. I don't know what we'll do." My heart sank. My mind flashed back to the dog in traffic. Good intentions with the career I had chosen, but I saw the negative impact my decision had.

The lesson stuck with me more this time. No matter how good your intention is, there will always be consequences for someone.

We all try to justify the impact of our actions. If I hadn't pulled the funding, would someone else have? Maybe. But you still must accept responsibility for the damage you leave in your path of intention. There will be impact, and you can't always control the impact as much as you can control your intention.

Eventually, I thought that maybe I could control the impact more if it were on my own terms. I realized I needed to be able to align my work with my beliefs. I wanted to do things in the community in the areas that I saw as critical. I wanted more control.

During the pandemic, I felt helpless, like many, and I was thinking about the state of St. Louis. I pondered the skills, talents, and privileges I could leverage. I decided to do something, try something.

My intentions for Fairstart were to build a company that levels the playing field for people to access better jobs. Remove the barriers, make the connections, and improve hiring diversity for companies. It felt like a win-win, and I would have greater control over the impact.

At first it seemed to work. People were getting jobs. I was hopeful; people were hopeful. But, like any startup, there were failures. The stakes were higher, though. We could perpetuate bias and turn employers away from innovation, thereby hurting the community I was trying to help. This time I recognized the need to pause. I didn't want to get to that gut-wrenching unintended impact moment that I knew all too well.

You might be blazing through the world guided by passion and clutching your intention. Being aware of your impact doesn't mean you have to stop. However, every once in a while, take a breather and see what you've left behind. What's happening on the peripheral? Is it what you intended? Do you need to pivot, or tweak? Also, sometimes you look back and realize that your impact was more powerful than you could have imagined.

I once spent no more than fifteen minutes giving advice to a young man who desperately needed a job. When I hung up, I didn't give it any thought. My intent was simply to motivate him to update his resumé and move on with my busy day. He called me a few weeks later and told me how that short conversation completely shifted his confidence and how he approached his job search. He was finally able to get a job that was changing his life.

Intention matters. Impact can matter more. Check your impact.

Maureen Hergenroether is married to her high school sweetheart, is a mother to three children and one fur baby, and resides in Defiance, Missouri. Born and raised in the St. Louis area, she has more than fifteen years of experience across numerous sectors including health services, travel, technology, nonprofit, and financial services. She is a senior leader in social responsibility, corporate philanthropy, and diversity & inclusion with an emphasis in communications. She is passionate about social equity, and enjoys public speaking and community building. In her spare times she loves horseback riding, spending time with friends, and supporting her children's hobbies.

Kimberly Rayford

Staying on the Path

"Go confidently in the direction of your dreams! Live the life you've imagined. As you simplify your life, the laws of the universe will be simpler."
—*Henry David Thoreau*

As I set out on this journey to talk about how I live my life with intention, I thought it would be best if I found a good working definition of "intention." The best I could find comes from The Britannica Dictionary: "The thing that you plan to do or achieve: an aim or purpose." While adequate and efficient in defining the term, it seemed too sterile and lacked a recognition of everything that is required to live an intentional life. I created my own definition of intention that is a more comfortable fit for my story: Set your goal, define your path, draw a map in pencil, set out on your journey, and be prepared for roadblocks and detours along the way. The detours and roadblocks gave me some trouble, but more about that later.

From a young age I knew my end goal in life: I wanted to be a scientist. At first, I didn't really know what a "scientist" was, but my father was one. He was an amazing human being, and I wanted to be just like him. My innocent, unformed mind had no idea how the journey toward this goal would unfold, but I started on my version of "the path."

I always had a curiosity about how things work and why things happen. I'm a question asker and will not rest until I get the answer, or at least an explanation, that makes sense. I was fortunate to have parents who were very supportive of my dreams but kept me grounded as well. They instilled a work ethic in me and would not accept excuses for laziness or bad grades, ever. When I was young, I thought they were way too strict or hard on me. In hindsight, I realized that what they were doing was helping draw the map I needed to reach my goal. They prepared me to expect excellence in myself and not settle for less than my best.

They insisted that I get involved in activities that did not involve studying science. I didn't understand what they were trying to teach me or what the purpose was. I wanted to do science, so I didn't see how dance lessons or learning an instrument had anything to do with that goal, or where those activities fit on the map that was beginning to take shape. I "knew best," and I was pretty determined to do things my way and not spend time practicing an instrument I didn't care to learn. After my parents grounded me a couple of times, I realized that maybe they knew what they were talking about. Again, hindsight is the best educator, and as an adult I now understand.

My pencil-drawn map started to become permanent ink right before I entered high school. I vividly remember the conversation like it was yesterday. My parents sat me down the night before my first day of high school and told me something that both scared me and gave me courage at the same time. They said that I was entering a very academically competitive school, and I wouldn't be the only smart girl in class anymore. There would be other smart girls as well, and it was now my job to continue to work hard and do my best. That wasn't the scary part. We chose my school for the specific reason that it was an all-girl school that expected academic excellence from its students as they educated girls to be leaders. The scary part came next. They told me that while they thought I was special to them, not everyone would feel the same way, and I had to develop a thick skin—quickly. I was a little naïve and didn't think I would have to deal with any of that. I was lucky that I could store that nugget of wisdom for another day. I spent four years picking my classes carefully with an eye to becoming a scientist. By this time, I had a firm grip on what a scientist was.

Then, I faced my first detour, which later became a roadblock. My father, who was my champion and mentor, was diagnosed with cancer. At the time, we thought he would fight this battle with his quiet strength and win. It looked like that was going to be the outcome as he continued his scientific career while living with his illness. I still remember the pride on his face when I was inducted into the National Honor Society, performed in our high school musicals, and when I received my diploma at graduation. I miss that smile to this day.

On to the next step on my path: college. I reluctantly went away to school. My father's cancer battle had taken a turn for the worse and I wanted to stay home; I had even been accepted by a university I could commute to. He wouldn't hear of it. He knew that I needed that opportunity to experience the independence that would help me develop my thick skin. I pulled that nugget out of storage because it was time to use it.

Then, I experienced my second detour. It had never occurred to me that someone would look at me and decide that I didn't belong somewhere based on my race and gender; my intention map didn't have a direction for that. I worked hard and did well in my classes freshman year. I began sophomore year excited by the prospect of building on everything I had learned. I selected my semester schedule with the sole purpose of advancing toward my goal. As I stepped into one of my classes, the professor took one look at me and said, "Oh, you must be in the wrong place." I replied that I was on his roster and had completed the course prerequisites. He rolled his eyes and said that he would check with my advisor, but I could stay for the day.

In that moment, that thick skin formed and protected me as I sat down and waited for class to start. When I arrived for the next class, he had verified my eligibility to attend. Then something unexpected happened. My fellow students were so outraged by how I'd been treated that they held back on answering questions so this professor was forced to call on me in class. After class, a group of them pulled me aside and invited me to their study group. I loved the support and built some friendships that have lasted to this day. It was also the first time that I realized my journey on the intentional path did not have to be a solitary one. I could allow some fellow travelers to accompany me. As an only child, I wasn't one to ask for help or show any type of weakness. I then understood that asking for help wasn't a sign of weakness but rather a higher level of self-awareness.

I hit my first big roadblock around this time. My father lost his battle with cancer, and I went into an absolute spiral. I had lost my guidepost, and my grades suffered. I was also tormented with a sense of guilt that I'd missed the last two years of his life by being away at college. It took what seemed like forever to recover and allow myself to remember the things he taught me. My grades suffered, and I didn't know how I was going to pull myself out of it.

I recovered eventually, finished college, and took the next step on my path. I got my dream first job and could feel my father's pride even though he wasn't there to express it. There were things I didn't expect— some good, some not so good. However, whatever I faced in that first Big Girl Job prepared me to continue my path in science and to reach my goal. Along the way I also discovered that I had an interest in law and was fortunate to pursue a degree in that field as well. That new skill set has contributed to my career in a variety of valuable ways.

Intention means different things to different people. Here are some ways I found intention or purpose:

9. Have a goal

10. Chart your path

11. Draw your map in pencil

12. Be prepared for detours and roadblocks

13. Gather your fellow travelers and ask for help and advice

14. Stay the course

It's your journey; find your intention and own it.

Kimberly Rayford is a regulatory science study director at Bayer Crop Science, a 2020 graduate of the Focus St. Louis CORO Women in Leadership Program, and a 2022 graduate of Washington University School of Law. She is a native St. Louisan who enjoys traveling and giving back to her community by supporting or volunteering for several nonprofit organizations including RUNG for Women, the St. Louis Zoo, and Cultural Festivals. Kimberly is a firm believer in the power of mentoring and providing guidance and support to future leaders who are looking to develop their talent and move forward into their ideal roles.

Stephanie Enger-Moreland

Finding My Way to Helping Others

From a young age, we're often asked, "What do you want to be when you grow up?" I recently asked my five-year-old this question, mainly for the purpose of this chapter. As he twirled around our living room, he said, "A trashman. I want to drive a recycle truck." I love this answer because at school he's learning about recycling and the environment. I'll be interested to see what he says as he enters high school, or later what he decides.

If someone had asked me what I wanted to be when I was five, I wonder what I would have said all those years ago. Perhaps a ballerina or a princess? At one point, I wanted to be a professional soccer or basketball player. But I was never at that level of play. I remember wanting to be on Broadway, a family law attorney, a physical therapist, and, lastly, what I originally went to school for, a high school history teacher. None of those are what my career path came to be. I always admired those who knew what they wanted to be from a young age and succeeded in following it. Their intention was clear and direct. Mine was foggy and uncertain.

After attending my first semester of college studying secondary education, I quickly learned this was not for me. For starters, students had to dedicate the last semester to student teaching, and not have a job. I couldn't do that, as I needed to work to support paying for college. So I took psychology, sociology, and criminology courses because I have always found the human brain fascinating. All of it was interesting, but, still, nothing intrigued me enough to dedicate four years to it. Eventually, I found a degree that melded my love of psychology with business: Organizational Leadership. I earned a minor in Criminology, and though I had no discipline to join the police academy, I wanted to support, serve, and advocate for victims. There it was, all those years earlier before I realized it myself, my intention to support and assist others.

I didn't have a goal for what I wanted to do with my life. It was frustrating at times to see where I fit in the scope of it all. What eventually shifted was a trip to the Gulf Coast. Through Maryville University's "alternative spring break," I served as part of a small group of students who spent the week in Pensacola, Florida, building a house for the local Habitat for Humanity. The sweet spot was being able to stay on the beach, a kind of reward for our hard work. During spring break, in my sophomore year, I signed up, not knowing a soul on the trip. Quickly, friend bonds formed, and this trip turned the direction of my life around.

As the frame and the walls of the home took shape, the structure became more visible. By the end of the week, all exterior walls were up, there was a roof with shingles, and windows were being installed. What had been a pile of construction materials became a home. Seeing the house take shape made me realize what I wanted to do in life: I wanted to help people. I was building a home for a first-time homebuyer who deserved to have a safe space of their own.

It would take several years after I graduated to fully grasp what "helping people" meant to me. I knew what I didn't want to do. I didn't want to continue with a job that didn't spark interest or joy. I was still working at a computer software company. It was a good company, but I wasn't going anywhere. It was a "boys' club," and there was me, who could dance circles around some of them. The push I needed came when

I lost my job due to downsizing. This change got me looking at my life and career. But "helping people" was very broad and could be taken in many different directions. I had a broad goal in mind, but it was tricky to find the next steps.

In setting my sights, I considered: How did I want to assist people, who did I want to help, and where was I going to begin? I started by researching master's programs in St. Louis and found a Master's in Nonprofit Administration program. I applied and got accepted to start the upcoming spring semester. After meeting with an advisor, it was clear to both of us I had zero experience in nonprofit. I had assisted with a couple of things as an undergrad, but I had no connections to the sector.

And so, I began climbing the ladder to gain experience and get my foot into the nonprofit world, a world that was completely foreign to me. My advisor told me prior to starting the master's program that I needed to get involved to understand the sector better. I joined a new young professionals' board for a local organization I had fundraised for in my undergrad. I started the master's program in January 2011, and joined the young professional board the same year, but didn't land my first nonprofit job until a year and a half later. I was very discouraged; I wasn't getting interviews because of my lack of experience.

Then I got an interview at a relatively new organization. Maybe seven years old, this nonprofit supported school kids by outfitting them with uniforms, school supplies, and much more. The job was for a warehouse manager, but it included managing inventory and volunteers. I had done inventory work! Finally, I had the experience a nonprofit was looking for.

By the third interview, I met with the hiring manager and the cofounder, who was also the executive director. I was offered the job, but it came with a serious pay decrease. At the time, it was a sacrifice I was willing to make. I finally got my foot in the door! The job gave me the experience and the opportunity to learn the basics of nonprofit work. For example, I attended a strategic operations meeting where I felt like a fish out of water. I learned about funding, and how donors and volunteers can support but also at times be harmful to an organization. As a warehouse manager, was I "helping people"? Indirectly, yes. My experience with this organization shifted how I viewed what programs and areas I wanted to work in. I finished my degree the following year and was offered a new position at the organization. For a variety of reasons, I decided to move on. But I am forever grateful to them for taking a chance on me.

The story doesn't end there; in fact, it's just the beginning. Recently, I saw a former supervisor, Erin. She was one of the best team leaders I had ever been a part of. We talked about various opportunities in St. Louis, and she was looking for a development director. I boldly said, "You should consider me." I was a little shocked that I said it, but out it came. She had someone she was interviewing, but kindly said she would keep it in mind. A few months later she became CEO of a new organization, and she called and asked, "I remember you said you were interested in development; we're looking for a Chief Development Officer, would you be interested in the position?"

My view of how I could help people shifted, and I realized it didn't have to be in direct service working with clients. I could raise money to support those who need assistance most. My intention to support and assist others never wavered. It was there, just taking different forms along the way.

After more than ten years in nonprofit, my career of working with underserved populations changed, as did where I wanted to land in an organization. Helping others has looked like advocating on policy at our state's capital, meeting with the Chief of Staff of our congresswoman regarding laws taking shape in DC. Helping others has looked like sitting beside a client as she tells her story of overcoming obstacles to ensure her children have a roof over their head. Helping others has been taking a stage to invite guests to give money to a worthy cause. Helping others has been learning about a genetic aortic condition, and the best way to speak to doctors to support their needs. Today, helping others is raising funds for children and families who seek and need mental health support because their family is facing the trauma of divorce. As a child of divorce and as a stepparent, this is a full circle moment for me.

What I've learned and want others to know is that the path to answering the question "What do I want to be when I grow up?" is not linear. Our intentions and views shift as we learn and grow throughout our lives. Our purposes can also shift based on life changes, situations, and circumstances. It's OK to not have it all figured out by a certain age. We compare ourselves and our lives to those we see on our TV or on social media. But real life is full of peaks, valleys, and winding roads.

While my path wasn't as clear as the paths of the people I envied all those years ago, the intention of my career came exactly when I needed it: on a hot day in Florida, with my arms hurting from hammering the frame of a house.

Stephanie Enger-Moreland has spent more than ten years in the nonprofit sector serving St. Louis families. Currently, she is the Chief Development Officer for Kids In The Middle, a mental health agency that supports children and families through divorce and separation. Her career experience has focused on volunteerism, programs, advocacy, and fundraising. Stephanie is an unapologetic guilt-free working mom; it's where she feels most creative. She is a native St. Louisan, born and raised. She earned her Master's in Nonprofit Administration from Lindenwood University in 2013. Since then, she's been lending her expertise to support organizations helping those in vulnerable populations.

Stephanie and her husband, Chris, reside in Fenton with their son and two dogs. She is a "bonus" mom to two older daughters. When Stephanie isn't trying to figure out how to change the world, you can find her catching up on all her favorite housewives or sitting back watching the chaos of her home.

Lori Drury

Cultivating Intentional Relationships

The Journey

When I reflect on my life's journey and career, two words come to mind: intentional relationships. The phrase "It is not what you know, but who you know" is the consistent quote and theme of my life, education, and career journey. From growing up in a faith-filled Catholic home and forming close bonds with immediate and extended family, to living in a small town where I knew everyone, developing relationships has been the solid foundation for my life. I was taught how my faith foundation is the strongest relationship I will ever have in my life. My high school sweetheart and I met and later married because our families knew each other and shared similar values. Without that foundation, I would not be the person I am today.

My adult life centered around intentional relationships and connections. Since the beginning of my college career, I have been an avid networker. It all started at the University of Missouri in Columbia (Mizzou) when inquiring with a friend about how she obtained her student work-study job in sports marketing. After asking her for a referral, her department recommended me to the Mizzou football team for student work opportunities. My work ethic and commitment to the job showed I was trustworthy and responsible to take on leadership roles as a liaison for recruiting activities as well as working with the coaching staff. Collegiate sports, recruiting, and marketing all center around the building and cultivating of relationships. This role was the building block of learning how to interact with people, to relate to a diverse group of people and roles, and to build rapport with supervisors and people who were willing to connect me to future opportunities.

After I graduated from the University of Missouri, where my husband was also finishing his business degree, I secured my first marketing job at my alma mater working in alumni relations for the Trulaske College of Business, Office of Advancement. From working for the Mizzou football team and then transitioning to Mizzou's business school, the transition was all about the relationships I made within the Mizzou network. The role allowed me to work in event planning, graphic design, and donor and alumni relations. The relationships I formed within the college's alumni relationships meant that when I was moving to St. Louis to continue my career, I was able to call upon those acquaintances and fellow alumni to make the transition easy.

Relationships and intentionality led to my recruitment into commercial real estate from academics based on my professional interactions, culture fit, and ability to connect well with people. In my various roles with the firm, I refined my marketing and business development skills on teams helping to grow the firm from a regional footprint to a global leader after four name changes and three company mergers during my tenure. From academics to corporate, I learned the value of connecting with people, expanding my skills, and how important purpose is in your work. I reached a point where I realized I was missing something. I had a great job working for a fast-growing global firm with incredibly talented people, but it wasn't what I wanted or the purpose I was seeking.

Building Relationships

"'For I know the plans I have for you,' declares the Lord, 'plans to prosper you and not to harm you, plans to give you hope and a future.'" Jeremiah 29:11 (NIV)

In the commercial real estate industry, working with incredibly talented people across the nation and the globe in a variety of expertise, relationships are built during near-term projects and transitioned to long-term successes and teams. The people I met, worked with, and worked for modeled this in how they approached business. You never know when someone you know or someone you worked for will come back into your life and provide an opportunity—for advancement or as a detriment. You do not know who you will meet, how they will impact you, and the impact you make on them—positively or negatively. The mentors, sponsors, and friendships formed in my commercial real estate career are ultimately what led me to make a change. God was calling me out of corporate America. I never would have guessed it would be to work for a nonprofit. I left the firm to work with my first supervisor in corporate, who had left his executive career to start a nonprofit workplace ministry.

My history of forming relationships spanning decades translates perfectly into leading a nonprofit where building intentional relationships is how we serve people and support our mission. Biblical Business Training (BBT) helps people apply biblical principles to work through small-group Bible study. BBT provides resources to people seeking to connect their faith and work and creates sustainable funding to keep the studies, technology, and coaching free for groups. What I learned in business about being intentional with people means I listen to their needs, inform them of the offerings as a solution, and support them every step of the way to grow in faith and leadership for the Lord. God equipped me to use my talents and gain valuable skills over the years to apply them to a nonprofit setting. I did not predict this path. When I reflect on my journey with perspective, God guided my relationships, my roles, my skills, and my circumstances with intention.

My career journey through academics, then into commercial real estate, and now in a nonprofit was God directing my path to enhance my God-given skills and gifts to be able to serve a nonprofit well. I learned the value of connecting with people, expanding my skills, learning from others, and how important purpose is in your work. All the managers with admirable leadership traits—as well as those who could use improvement in my work history—shaped me into how I live, work, and lead today.

Relationships Beyond Business

Relationships are not only for business; building and sustaining relation-ships with God, your family, and your friends are of the utmost impor-tance. When the work is finished, who and what is left in your life?

Faith was a main part of my early life, although it grew quiet in my young adult years due to the pursuit of achievement, worldly distractions, and my own goals. However, I felt like I was missing something in my life and career journey. God never left me, and He directed my path no matter how aware of it I was or not. Life and work experiences drew me back to God and renewed my relationship to seek Him in all I do. I often wonder how much better of a daughter, sister, wife, mother, friend, and employee I could be if I would have kept God at the center of my journey. Now, my relationship with the Lord takes priority. Much like relationships with people, growing in relationship with God takes intention and work. It is the key to my longevity and legacy.

Self-care is often overlooked by women when caring for and serving others. It took me a while to realize that I cannot forget about myself. I need quiet time to myself to recharge and renew, and I intentionally schedule time for self-care. Next to God, my longest and future relationship lies inside me. The saying goes that we cannot fill up others from our empty cup. I cannot give from what I do not have within myself.

After ensuring my relationship with God and my inner self is in good standing, my family receives the most focus. "Family First" is my team's motto, and we hold each other accountable to it. My family is my greatest asset and will endure the path ahead with me. Establishing the bonds with my family when I was young taught me to create the same environment for my husband and children. Family is forever, and I invest my time with them with presence and focus.

What do intentional relationships look like? Making time to spend with others, being present when you're with them, and staying in contact are the cornerstones. Going out of your way to ask someone how they are doing, asking how you can pray for them, or simply listening means so much. Being intentional is a two-way street. If you are only taking from a relationship, it is not a fair relationship. Forming 360-degree relationships brings strength and longevity. As the scripture says, "When someone has been given much, much will be required in return; and when someone has been entrusted with much, even more will be required." Luke 12:48b (NLT) The same goes for being intentional through relationships. If you are blessed by someone or something, return the blessing without expecting anything in return, or pay it forward to someone else. We never know when you might need something, and someone will be there to return the favor. Serving others does not always mean you get to see the immediate gratification of the reward, but someday you'll be rewarded eternally.

Lori Drury is Executive Director and CEO of Biblical Business Training (BBT) and is dedicated to helping people apply biblical principles at work through providing group leaders with the curriculum, connectivity, and coaching to start a Bible study, and keeping those resources free for groups through fundraising. She served in every capacity for the organization: Bible study participant and group leader, donor, staff, and now as the leader. Lori brings marketing, business development, and brand awareness experience from her previous roles at Cushman & Wakefield, the University of Missouri, Robert J. Trulaske, Sr. College of Business, and entrepreneurship. Lori earned a Bachelor of Science in Business Administration with an emphasis in Marketing from the University of Missouri. In her spare time, outside of family and work, she volunteers her time with several professional and community organizations in St. Louis. She and her husband, Kory, have two young sons.

Lusnail Haberberger

Bringing *Familia* to Corporate America

I was born and raised in Caracas, Venezuela, surrounded by a loving family. Both my mother and my father were engineers, specializing in the same field. My mother was a brilliant leader who excelled rather quickly in her career, faster than my father. She worked for the governmental institution and was in charge of reviewing and approving the projects completed by my father's team. Forty years ago, in a very patriarchic society, this caused problems for my mother, not only at work but also at home. The engineering work environment for her was toxic. Women at that time were not respected as highly as their male counterparts, no matter what position they held in the hierarchy. My mother was often subjected to unprovoked, inappropriate jokes about "'handling" my father. As a result, she made the difficult decision to leave her successful engineering career and focus on raising her children and supporting her spouse.

I grew up watching my mother struggle with her decision to abandon her career. I witnessed her battle with mixed emotions and sometimes resenting my father, who had always respected her, adored her, and treated her like a queen. As life has it, we lost my father, our sole financial supporter, when I was fifteen. At this point, my mother, a stay-at-home mother of four children—two in college and two in high school—had been out of the workforce for fourteen years. Fearful and desperate to survive, she faced adversity and found a way to persevere. First, she used my father's death policy to invest in rental properties. Then she pivoted and reinvented herself. Soon, she was able to earn an income stable enough to pay for our private high school education, our home, our unforgettable family vacations, and, later, my educational journey in the United States. I am forever thankful my mother was able to recognize her strength, her grit, and her resilience. Through her experience, I set an intention for my professional and personal life that has profoundly impacted my family and my employees. In many ways, I now live the life my mother dreamed of.

The struggles I observed in my family deeply impacted me. I decided I wanted to study as hard as possible so that I could become a great engineer and someday change the perspectives surrounding women in the engineering field. A driven student, I earned a bachelor's degree in electrical engineering, followed by a master's in electrical engineering and then an MBA. Shortly afterward, I was on the career path I had imagined. Then I gave birth to my first son, José.

I started to feel conflicted, as my own mother had felt. How could I be the "perfect" mother and reach my fullest potential in a career that I love? I pushed through my doubts and continued to excel in my career. However, after my second son, Luca, was born, just fourteen months after my first, the dilemmas in my mind became more and more overwhelming. I did not feel comfortable taking time away from work to take my boys to their doctors' appointments, or to pick them up from school on early dismissal days, or to stay home whenever one of them had a fever. I wanted to attend my children's class parties and school performances, but I also wanted my colleagues to know that I was as reliable and dedicated as ever.

Warranted or not, each time I left work for any reason associated with my children, I felt like I was letting my team down. I worked in a male-dominated field, and I did not see my colleagues leaving work early or working from home (mind you, this was before the pandemic) to tend to their familial obligations. I did not like feeling guilty for wanting to prioritize my career and my role as a parent, especially when I knew I was fully capable of doing both.

Throughout the years, I have noticed that women, especially women of color, are underrepresented in the engineering world, and even more so in the entrepreneurship world and in C-suite positions. Why are we underrepresented? Why can't a woman feel like a valued member of her team and rightfully care for her own children? Why don't companies do more to support their employees' well-being and work-life balance? Why are there pay discrepancies? Why do so many people feel the same way as me, yet there is so little progress?

I grew tired of asking why. I decided I had to focus on the "Why Nots." If I wanted to redefine the idea of professionalism for both women and men and take control of my narrative, I needed to take action. I was determined to demonstrate that professionals can equally focus on their careers and home lives, and that companies should, in fact, choose to facilitate that balance. This became my motivation for starting my own business.

Familia means "family" in Spanish, and it is at the center of how I live my life as a wife, a mother, a friend, and a colleague. It is also how I lead my team at LUZCO Technologies. To me, familia represents strength, support, acceptance, disagreements, love, and a genuine respect for each other. My intent to apply the idea of family in a corporate environment is not groundbreaking. There are several successful leaders who try to exemplify this. However, the concept remains difficult to establish in so many industries because, historically, we have been told that a balance between one's work and home life is not achievable. Thankfully, professionals like me are starting to ask "Why not?"

I believe it is a family-nurturing environment that allows each one of us to be our authentic selves. I also believe this authenticity translates into innovation and value creation for our team and for our clients. I made it my goal to foster a workplace culture that promotes genuine care for each other, one that embraces diversity, innovation, and leadership development, as well as family life.

LUZCO grew from a team of two to a familia of more than 100 employees in its first six years. I attribute our success to our familia-focused culture—one that was built with intention. Our culture is embedded in who we are and how we operate. Every decision we make aligns with our mission. When I founded LUZCO, I wanted to create an environment where parents, caregivers, sons, daughters, and partners did not have to worry about the perception that being present with their loved ones degraded the quality of their work or their branding/reputation as professionals. I wanted to build a company where life-work balance is not just a slogan, but rather an intention that is fully supported by our executive and leadership teams. Today, all new LUZCO employees understand that there is a learning curve for every new position (so someone joining our company with no prior industry experience might take a little more time), but once they have adjusted, they are granted autonomy in how they manage their schedules.

I also practice what I preach to set an example for my employees. I intentionally block my calendar every morning and afternoon so I can drop my boys off at school and pick them up and hear about their day. Sometimes my children and/or my dogs accompany me to the office. My employees and clients know that even though I do not have a traditional work schedule, they can rely on me to stay responsive, to solve problems, and to meet every project demand. I understand that I can prioritize my schedule in a way I can succeed as a parent and as a professional, and I trust that my employees can do the same. I want them to take advantage of their freedom.

I found my calling in trying to break the barriers that ended the careers of so many brilliant engineers, like my mother. My vision is to show the world that well-balanced working women do exist, and that an immigrant woman of color can achieve a successful engineering career, redefine norms, and be a present mother and partner. To me, LUZCO is a representation of my vision. It is my proof that perspectives can be challenged and that change only happens when individuals take action.

My mother taught me that life is a journey. Unfortunate circumstances occur, and unexpected curveballs get thrown our way. However, every day, we have the gift of controlling our mindset—the way we interpret the things we cannot control. Our mindset plays an important role in how we want to move forward in life. To me, being intentional means making tough decisions and creating the best resolutions while staying true to our beliefs. In the face of adversity, I try to refer back to the "Why Nots." It makes each decision process smoother and more efficient, and it helps me stay true to LUZCO's values. Leading from the heart, always doing the right thing even when someone is not watching, and caring for each other will enable us to build a better community all around.

Lusnail Rondón Haberberger, PE, PMP, is the founder and CEO of LUZCO Technologies, LLC. She harnessed her electrical engineering and project management skills to launch LUZCO Technologies in 2017. Under her leadership, LUZCO grew from a one-person business into an award-winning, certified woman-owned and minority-owned boutique engineering firm, with offices in Missouri and New York.

As a Venezuelan-born mother of two, Lus has made it her mission to expand resources for local youth, immigrants, and women interested in STEM careers and entrepreneurship. She heads LUZCOmmunity, a team of LUZCO employees dedicated to local philanthropy, and has served on the board of Casa De Salud since 2018.

Lus's portfolio of awards includes: *Enterprising Women* magazine's 2020 Enterprising Women of the Year Award, the 2020 *Small Business Monthly* Top Women Business Owners Award, the *St. Louis Business Journal's* 2021 C-Suite Awards, and the *St. Louis Business Journal's* 2022 Most Influential Business Woman.

Dr. Jade D. James-Halbert

Divine Intention

When I think about intention, I think of words like deliberate, purposeful, and determined. Some would use words such as fortunate, lucky, coincidental, or even accidental to describe their interpretation of my success. However, when I reflect on my life, I would describe it as a testimony. I'm often overwhelmed when I think of God's I.N.T.E.N.T.I.O.N. for my life: God Intended Never To Ever Neglect Thee In spite Of Negativity. He provided grace, mercy, and love every step of the way. Allow me to elaborate.

I am the second-born child of my parents, Lorna Turner-James and Charles Edward James Senior. My mother is an educator, and my father was a police officer. Each were born and raised in a family that expected excellence in life's pursuits. Excellence doesn't mean perfection. Excellence doesn't mean lack of trial or tribulation. Excellence means giving your best ability to achieve the goal you've set forth and allowing your gifts to make room for you. Excellence means not giving up when it gets hard. Excellence means if the traditional route has a boulder in the middle of the path, then seeking an alternative route, and if none exists, creating one. Excellence means identifying your goals, and your family and friends supporting those goals. Excellence means a learned mentality that you teach your children. Excellence means intentionally teaching your children these same values and supporting their achievements.

My parents divorced before I was two years old. I was raised by a single mother. My father was tragically killed in the line of duty one month before my tenth birthday.

With God's direction, my mother continued to instill excellence in all aspects of my life. My formal education and my spiritual foundations were rooted in Catholicism. Religion and its perception thereof can be rather controversial. To this day, I remain unapologetically Black and Catholic in America. Through Catholicism, my family was gifted with intention: Inspiration, Nurturing, Tenacity, Everlasting love, Neighbors, Toughness, Ingenuity, Optimism, and Numerous memories. Black Catholicism gave me love, laughter, community, education, and life. My mother was able to find peace and love from the family that adopted her after she lost her biological mother at age fourteen. She was engaged with her biological family as well. I believe it was God's intention for her to have two families' love, which filled the space left empty by the loss of her mother. These three families helped my mother instill excellence and community in her children. I was about five when I voiced my desire to be a doctor. These families united in their mission to love, nurture, and support the foundation necessary to achieve this goal.

I felt socially and emotionally awkward when I started high school, although I was very clear about my academic and professional goals. I attended Cardinal Ritter College Prep High School where the entire staff was intentional about students' success during and after high school. The three-fold mission of academic excellence, faith development, and leadership was intended to set its students and graduates up for success no matter what career path they chose. The faculty and staff at Cardinal Ritter could often see excellence in students who demonstrated everything but excellence. They would not only help you see your personal excellence but demand it from you. It was just the right dose of tough love sprinkled with mercy and grace, giving awkward, obnoxious adolescents the ability to grow and flourish at a time when zero-tolerance policies didn't teach the rules, yet the student was expected to be perfect in knowing and executing them. It was Cardinal Ritter's purpose to nurture, love, and mold you into an adult with intention: Integrity, Nimbleness, Tenacity, Endurance, Notable, Tenderness, Innovation, Outstanding, and a Noteworthy foundation.

From high school, I went on to complete an undergraduate degree at Fisk University and my medical education at Meharry Medical College. Because of my early years, my path to medicine was well defined. Everyone I encountered personally and professionally supported my journey. From educational scholarships to accelerated courses, there was no stopping this train. For every setback, there was a comeback even stronger. There was grit and resilience, before these were commonplace words used in today's vernacular. It wasn't until medical school that I needed to tap into my own intention. During med school, I had a moment when I wondered why "everyone" wanted me to be a doctor so badly. I was taking an anatomy and physiology class, and the work was overwhelming. The information didn't seem hard; it was just a lot at one time and there was no way around reading, reviewing, and working with your group. This was the first time I was challenged in this manner, and I was ready to throw in the towel. I wanted to get off that train at the next exit. The challenge seemed insurmountable. I wasn't sure if this was for me.

It was in that moment that God reminded me that this whole thing was my idea and everyone else was supporting me. God reminded me this was something I voiced around age five and never looked back. I never considered anything else. My village and my support had not disappeared; it had been rearranged. There were new villagers now, but the old villagers remained steadfast in their intention: Irreplaceable Nurturing,

Toughness, Energy, Notion of prayer, Tenderness, Integral Optimism, and Nonnegotiable faith. The new villagers were my study partners, fellow classmates, professors, and future colleagues. These were the people with whom I would now travel on the next part of life's journey—the same people who would only lock arms if you were going to ride this train to the end, not just the next exit.

It was at this moment and this time that I needed to be reminded of my own intention. Excellence doesn't mean easy. Excellence doesn't mean there won't be trials and tribulations. Excellence doesn't mean it won't get hard. Excellence means identifying your own goals, and that your family and friends will support those goals. Excellence means to give your best ability to achieve the goal you've set forth and allow your gifts to make room for you. In other words, intention: (I couldn't) Imagine Not Taking Every Notion To Influence Others Nationally. My passion and my intention was healthcare, and this was no time to exit the train. This would be the first of many instances in which my intention was tested and recalled.

In 2020, the world was faced with a global pandemic. As a healthcare provider it was scary, overwhelming, and devastating—both personally and professionally. Having been a physician for twenty years, I gave serious consideration to exiting the train again. I saw colleagues retire. I saw colleagues succumb to the disease. I saw my family devastated. I was devastated. I saw a healthcare system that I so passionately loved (though I was no longer naïve to its dark side) nearly crumble. I often reflected, and it was somber.

Though painstakingly obvious, reflection was cathartic. I had long aspired to engage with medicine in a different manner. The healthcare system and I weathered the storm of the pandemic, and I saw an opportunity to pivot. I leaned into the opportunity with both conflict and optimism: conflicted about leaving the patients who I had taken care of in a system of insufficient resources and social determinants, but optimistic about bridging some of the gaps that make social determinants a barrier and working to improve the wider system as opposed to one patient at a time. This was indeed a pivotal moment, but not the way I had envisioned. When this opportunity was no longer available, I was stuck in the proverbial hallway. I had closed the door behind me, and the door in front of me was no longer open. The hallway was filled with devastation, disappointment, despair, deceit, and anger. Accepting the emotional rollercoaster before me, there was also an immediate reminder of God's intention for me: *Intended Never To Ever Neglect Thee In spite Of Negativity.* In the midst of the emotional chaos, there was a calmness, a reflection, a recall of MY INTENTION: *Imagine Not Taking Every Notion To Influence Others Nationally.* "Surely goodness and mercy shall follow me all the days of my life" —Psalms 23

I am no longer in the hallway. Nowadays, I am moving with intention. I am no longer coasting through life's standard pathways. I am forever grateful for grace and mercy. Together, these twins have helped me to navigate my foundational values of love, life, community, education, and excellence. Without them, I would still be in the angry hallway. I am intentionally forging ahead with G.R.I.T.

Dr. Jade D. James-Halbert, MD MPH is a board-certified obstetrician/ gynecologist, serving uninsured and underinsured communities in the Greater St. Louis Area for the last twenty years. Currently, she is Chair of the Department of Obstetrics and Gynecology and an OB Hospitalist for SSM DePaul. Clinically, she has worked as a women's health physician for People's Health Center, Myrtle H. Davis Comprehensive Health Center, CareSTL Health, and SSM DePaul. She served as Deputy Director of Research and Medical Services for St. Louis County Department of Health, and on the boards of the National Centers for Missing and Exploited Children African American Advisory Board, the Regional Health Commission Provider Services Advisory Board, St Louis Area Foodbank, Riverview West Florissant Development Corporation, Girl Scouts of Eastern Missouri, Youth Achiever's Foundation, Logan University, HEAL Center for the Arts, and the Missouri Board of Registration for the Healing Arts. She is a certified RETAIN Parental Leave Coach. Her training includes Postpartum Support International and Heartland protocol for perinatal mood and anxiety disorders.

Tina Asher

Own Your Day

86,400. That's how many seconds are in a day. How intentional are you about making every second count? I wasn't.

One of the hardest lessons I've learned over time is to live in the present. I spent a lifetime of hoping for the next best thing. Get a driver's license, become an adult, get the nice car and the nice home, get married, have kids, get the promotion—you know, the "checklist for a good life" syndrome. But with that comes the worry. What if I don't or can't get those items, then what?

I decided to pour myself into my work, and the hustle began. I was so accustomed to cramming and jamming my schedule that my calendar looked like it was in a war zone. My blood pressure increased just looking at it. Each morning, the pattern continued. I buckled up and headed for the races, chasing one appointment after the next until it was time to collapse on my pillow for a short night's rest.

This went on for three decades until I lost my job. Although I had quite the ride during my career of making great friends, winning award trips, receiving promotions, owning bigger homes and faster cars, it took a toll on my personal life. My first marriage crumbled, and my life at home with the kids became a blur. I kept chasing the next best thing so we could "be better off." The price I paid for the chase cost me what I adored the most. My bank account was full, yet my soul was bankrupt.

As I wrote in my book, *Teetering, A Frazzled Overworked Person's Guide to Embrace Change and Find Balance*, "The people who cared the least about me got the most of me. And the people who cared the most about me got the least." The way I was living was not a good return on my investment.

I wanted a change. I realized this was the time to be intentional about owning my day so that life and work would complement each other. From that desire and intention, my business, Build U Up Consulting, was born.

My passion became a mission.

I was determined to help as many people as possible have better careers, be better bosses, or run better businesses so they can live better lives both at home and at work. The focus has always been to build others up by helping them identify and use their God-given talents to live their days intentionally, becoming proactive instead of reactive in their activities. That's how they, and now you, can begin to own your day.

As a business consultant and career coach, most of my clients have a similar pattern. Maybe you can relate? They want more out of life, they're tired of doing meaningless work that's not valued or appreciated, they haven't received the professional development they want to get ahead, and they're trying to run their business or team in a way that is profitable, fun, and impactful. Yet they don't know how to do it.

Although each situation is unique, you can all learn how to own your day. One of the first steps is to list all your commitments. How often do you say "yes" to things you think you want to be part of, only later to regret having said yes in the first place? It's like going to a restaurant when you're hungry and ordering everything on the menu that sounds good and by the time the main course is served, you're already full.

A while back I was overcommitted, and it provoked me to write an article about it. Here's an excerpt from that article:

"Last month I had to put myself on a "yes" diet. No more filling my plate with saying yes to things that aren't in alignment with what's best for me, my family, or my lifestyle. I had a large helping of overcommitments on my plate and it bogged me down. I noticed I became reactive instead of proactive and I wasn't enjoying the things I had said "yes" to. I decided to go on a on a diet and cut some things out of my life."

Maybe you're in that spot right now. Endless opportunities appear to be part of fundraisers, networking events, becoming a board member, kid's activities, family obligations—oh, and don't forget the demands of your job. It's exhausting. It's time to stop saying yes to things that don't serve you and start owning your day with intention.

In my younger years I was a victim of FOMO. You know, the Fear Of Missing Out?

Lately, I've realized that to own my day, I have to flip the script. Now I live in the world of FOMO as I define it: Fear Of Making Overcommitments.

It was important for me to be intentional about what I committed my time to, and that the commitment lined up with my core values. Determining your values is key to being intentional and making wise choices. For me, my core values are God, family, and career, in that order. For you it may be something different.

When you say "yes" to a commitment, run it through the "Could I?" versus "Should I?" test. Let's face it, people ask you to join a group, volunteer your time, or be part of an organization because they see something in you. You're skilled, talented, and they think you could do a good job at whatever the commitment is. So, the "Could I?" part is easy. Of course you can do it. The real question becomes "Should I?" do it?

Most of my clients get caught in this trap: they think they can fit one more thing on their plate because something else will be finished soon, so they agree to add it on. When that happens, there's a price to pay, and the cost can be high. It's a drain on your energy, your quality time with loved ones, and on your capacity to own your day.

Take inventory of your commitments. List all the commitments you've said yes to. Next, look over your list and assign an emotion to it. Is it a Smiley Face (love doing this), is it a Mediocre Face (could live with or without it), or is it a Sad Face (dread doing this)? Now, begin to eliminate all the Sad Face items, and then move onto the Mediocre Face items. Evaluate how much energy you are using to participate in something that doesn't fill you up with excitement. If it doesn't excite you, then consider removing that commitment.

I've created three easy steps to follow to avoid overcommitting:

REFLECT:

- When and why did you commit to this?

- Choosing to say yes to something in the future because you think you have time later is a trap. There will always be something on your calendar begging for your attention.

- If you aren't prepared to say yes as if it would begin tomorrow, then it's a clear no. The things you're passionate about will be a no-brainer to agree to, and you'll want to do them right away.

RESET:

- Examine your core values. Make sure your decisions are in alignment with who you say you want to be.

- What are your most important priorities in life? Will this new position, activity, or program enhance your priorities in life or hinder them?

- Decisions become clearer when you are in alignment with your core values and priorities.

RECHARGE:

- Recognize that if you say no, you're doing the program, activity, or organization a favor by saying no when you're not 100 percent committed to it.

- When you know it's not the right thing for you to do and you pass on it, the opportunity opens for someone who's eager to serve. You've helped them more with your no than you would have with a half-hearted yes.

- Once you've lightened the load and only committed to the things you care the most about, you'll serve at a deeper level and feel more connected to your cause or position.

What will you take off your plate to lighten your load and stay energized?

Life has taught me to live in the present, and, if I'm truthful, it's a constant struggle. It's an intentional practice for me to stay present. Focusing on what makes me a better person for myself, my family, and my clients is my top priority. By not overcommitting, I can stay more at peace and be present. My daily prayer and intention to live my best life is to ask myself, "How can I serve God with the gifts he's given me, have time for rest, and be my best for those around me?" Once I stopped overcommitting, I began to own my days, weeks, and even my year. Now it's your turn. How will you spend your 86,400 seconds to own your day?

Tina Asher is the founder and president of Build U Up Consulting and author of *Teetering: A Frazzled, Overworked Person's Guide to Embrace Change and Find Balance.* She helps busy professionals and business owners get out of the rat race and build on a career that they love.

Tina works with individuals and businesses to meet their talent management needs and personal career goals with patented solutions and programs. Her multiple certifications include: Professional Behavior (DISC) Analyst (CPBA); Professional Driving Forces Analyst (CPDFA); Professional TriMetrixHD Analyst (CPHDA); and Professional Emotional Quotient Analyst (CEQA).

Prior to opening her practice, Tina was a leader in the mortgage insurance and finance industry for more than thirty years. Her experience in the corporate world included roles in management, sales, marketing, operations, training, and customer service.

Tina's passion is encouraging others to reach their full potential while balancing a full and productive life. Tina is a woman of faith, mother to three young adults, and lives with her husband, Dan, in Missouri.

Dr. Roslyn Grant

A Legacy of Intention

"Never forget that intelligence rules the world and ignorance carries the burden. Therefore, remove yourself as far as possible from ignorance and seek as far as possible to be intelligent." —Marcus Garvey

My maternal grandmother was named Garvey, after Jamaican political activist Marcus Garvey. As a young girl, this quote exemplified how she lived her life. Though my grandmother only went to elementary school for a few years, she was one of the most intelligent women I ever knew. Growing up as a young Black girl in the 1920s and 1930s, she knew she wouldn't have the same educational opportunities as other girls her age, but she loved to read and had a phenomenal memory. So she read as often as she could, especially the Bible, often memorizing what she read. She could recite entire chapters of the Bible verbatim, often to the surprise of people who heard her. The acquisition of knowledge was very important to her, and she transferred the importance of education to her children.

My grandmother intentionally orchestrated my mother's life to give her the best opportunity to be whatever she wanted to be. She raised her with the intention of obtaining a high-quality education. She also took measures to shield her from negative influences and people who might have preconceptions about her . . . whether they be friend, family, or foe.

An example of this was when my mother was about seven or eight years old. My grandmother was a housemaid for various white families in the affluent neighborhoods of St. Louis, Missouri. One day, my grandmother brought my mother to work with her. My mother and the young daughter of the employer were playing together. The employer saw the children and said to my grandmother, "Oh, look, they get along so well. Maybe one day your daughter can work for my daughter." My grandmother finished her work that day and never returned. That was not the plan she had for her daughter. She refused to expose herself or her daughter to people who placed them in a category, regardless of their intention. So she removed herself from further interactions with that employer—no matter the consequences.

Years later, when my grandmother felt that the school my mother and her brother were assigned to attend wasn't the best educational option for them, she negotiated with the principal to place them in another school she believed was a better educational fit. Ultimately, my mother attended Sumner High School, the oldest Black high school west of the Mississippi. At the time, the school was the epitome of Black excellence. She also received a full scholarship to Homer G. Phillips School of Nursing in St. Louis. The nursing school was linked to Homer G. Phillips Hospital, which was internationally known as a state-of-the-art institution serving the region's Black residents. My mother went on to be a successful pediatric nurse, caring for children for more than thirty years until she retired.

The tenacity and fortitude of my grandmother raised the purposeful and determined woman who would ultimately become a wife and mother—my mother, Josie.

Train up a child in the way he should go, and when he is old, he will not depart from it. —Proverbs 22:6

As a Black family growing up in a majority white neighborhood, my brothers and I had many challenges that we endured on a regular basis: The fear when being taunted by a mob of neighborhood kids; the frustration of having to prove to the elementary school teacher that our family traveled around the United States every summer; the sadness of having the gym teacher as your square dance partner because none of the kids chose you; or the shame of wanting to be a different color because of the constant comments about your brown skin.

My mother instilled in my three brothers and me the courage and confidence needed to survive and thrive in the social and racial landscape. She also raised us with the intention to be educated, well-rounded, confident, and caring individuals. She believed a formal education was very important, but also believed in supplementing education with experiences. We were encouraged to be athletic and creative. We participated in sports and took music lessons. She taught us about prominent Africans and African Americans and their important work (because it wasn't taught in our school). We were very active in our church and were taught to thank God for everything we have and everything we do. She also introduced us to experiences outside of our normal circle, as we regularly visited museums and historical sites, caves, and national parks.

One of the most memorable traditions was when she would read books to us throughout the year, then take us on road trips during the summer to visit the locations where the books were set. This tradition transported me, my mom, dad, and brothers all over the United States. This allowed us to experience and respect different cultures, people, and points of view.

So when the mob of neighborhood kids came to our home looking for my brother, she guided all of us through a conversation that ultimately led to forgiveness. She taught us that a picture is better than a thousand words when she gave us the photos of our many family road trips across the United States to share at "show and tell." We also learned that our brown skin was beautiful and that it was not our fault if others were too blind to see it. The purposefulness and determination of my mother raised the woman of intention that I am today.

"I am the dream and the hope of a slave." —Maya Angelou

I am the fusion of the tenacity, fortitude, purposefulness, and determination of my mother, grandmother, and all the ancestors before me. I believe each generation should build on the success and strength of those who deferred or sacrificed their dreams (and sometimes their lives) so their descendants might have a better life. My mother and grandmother set things in place so I could realize my dreams and fulfill my purpose.

In his book, *Discover Your True North*, author Bill George wrote: "True North is your inner sense, or your calling, of what you want to accomplish in your life. It's a combination of your values, your beliefs, and your purpose." Family has always been the purpose behind my True North. It's what drives nearly everything I do. I live my life in this way because of the example epitomized by my mother and grandmother. They were intentional in preparing me for life, and, as the benefactor, I've been intentional about planning my life so I can pay it forward. This is my approach.

Make a Plan and Document It

One day, I came home from school to find my dad lying on the living room floor doing paperwork. I asked him what he was doing, and he explained that he was in a training class and the trainer had assigned homework. I was intrigued that someone could "make" my dad do homework. That's when I decided I wanted to be a corporate trainer. The next day, I did extensive research to find out more about this role. I talked with everyone I knew who was in the training business to obtain guidance on how to enter the field. Then I created the plan and documented what I needed to do to achieve my goal. I solicited leaders in the training field to mentor me to keep me on the right track. I had three mentors who I talked to every few months, who stayed updated on my progress. The documented plan kept me focused, and I was able to accomplish all the goals I set.

Align With the Right People

My grandmother knew that aligning with the wrong people could alter the direction of our lives, so she did everything she could to ensure her children had the right influences. I've done the same throughout my life.

It was important to me to align with the right people in my personal and professional life. The alignment was twofold. To "pay it forward," I mentored young men and women who needed help developing and preparing themselves for the future. I also aligned myself with people whose values were like mine. Therefore, we could support each other in achieving goals.

Don't Diverge From Your Core Values

Family and integrity are the two core values that rise to the top every time I do a values exercise. I consider these two values when making any major decision in my life.

One of the most important things a person can do is stay true to themselves, their values, and not stray from them—even if it's unpopular. If you stay true to yourself by living your values, you will have no guilt or regret for actions you've taken or decisions you've made.

My grandmother, Garvey, and mother, Josie, focused on family and made the best decisions for then, now, and the future. I am forever grateful for their tenacity, fortitude, purposefulness, and determination.

Though I focused on myself, my mother, and my grandmother in this chapter, it's important to note that my great-grandfather Ophelia, my grandfather David, and my father Roosevelt were all very present in raising, supporting, and loving these phenomenal women.

Dr. Roslyn Grant is Director of Organization Development for a large health system in Wisconsin. She serves as Executive Director of the Velt Foundation, an organization serving neighborhoods in North St. Louis. She is also the founder of Grant Performance Group LLC, a consulting company focusing on elevating the performance of people and organizations through development, alignment, engagement, and inclusion.

Roslyn has more than twenty years of experience in leadership development, strategic planning, organization development, and human resources. She is passionate about assuring individuals are equipped with the tools, resources, opportunities, and support required for success. She shares her knowledge and expertise with local and national faith-based and youth organizations, as well as several community boards and committees.

Roslyn holds a PhD in Organization Development from Benedictine University, a Master's degree in Management and Human Resources Development from Webster University, and a Bachelor's degree in Communications and Psychology from the University of Missouri.

Jessica Lopez-Liggett

Shaping Your Destiny, Defying Circumstances

My story is about the journey of a young woman who emerged from a lower socioeconomic background, became a mother at a young age, and defied the odds to forge a successful career. The journey exemplifies the profound impact intentionality can have on personal and professional growth by making deliberate choices to capitalize on the right opportunities. In a world full of uncertainty, remarkable determination is required to navigate obstacles and find a successful career path. Ultimately, the right amount of intentionality can lead to remarkable results, even in the face of adversity.

A clear path to success felt uncertain growing up in a lower socioeconomic family. My family's desire to provide a better life for themselves fueled my determination to rise above their circumstances. Growing up in the inner city of St. Louis, Missouri, where many areas are considered impoverished, my parents knew that wasn't the life they wanted for my brother and me. They didn't always have the means or resources to help them navigate, but their own determination and intentional decision-making led us out of that life and into one that was above where they started. I watched my parents work hard for what we had, with no support, and they faced numerous decisions with purpose and intention. They knew that every choice they made would move us either forward or backward. Thanks to my parents, the decision to be intentional in every aspect of life, including my career, became the cornerstone of my journey.

Being the child of parents who had a ninth-grade education and married at the young age of fifteen could have been seen as an insurmountable challenge. My parents understood the importance of education and pushed hard to ensure that I not only completed high school but went on to college. It seemed impossible at times. High school was never a question for me. I knew I would finish. However, where and how I finished was based on their decisions. Aware that the environment surrounding you shapes who you are, my family took a risk and moved me to a school in the Mehlville Public School District outside of our own neighborhood. They knew I would have access to a better education and more resources there. I envisioned this next chapter to be exciting, even though I did not have direction on the how's or why's to what I was doing. I leveraged resources, such as guidance counselors, at my high school. I am incredibly grateful to those resources because they helped to make my dream a reality.

Education was long recognized as a key factor in upward mobility throughout my childhood, so after I completed high school, I decided I would be the first in my family to take a leap into higher education. With the help from financial assistance and grants, my parents afforded me the opportunity to attend St. Louis Community College–Meramec. After junior college, I enrolled at the University of Missouri–St. Louis to obtain my bachelor's degree. Once again, I had to be resourceful and intentional with my means. Curiosity and determination led me to financial resources, and to cover what I couldn't afford, I chose faith over fear and took out student loans. I kept telling myself it would all work out, I just needed to keep putting one foot in front of the other.

During college, I was surprised by an unexpected pregnancy. Being a mother and a college student was seen as an insurmountable challenge, especially in the eyes of my father. I explained that the birth of my daughter Morgan would be motivation to further excel rather than a hinderance to my ambitions. My maternal responsibilities would further fuel my desire for professional growth. My daughter would be my motivation. If I was going to succeed, I would need to be intentional with time management, goal prioritization, and leveraging every resource available to pursue my bachelor's degree while working full time and raising my daughter. Balancing the demands of work, parenting, and academics required a tremendous amount of discipline and dedication. While many of my friends were out enjoying life as young twenty-somethings, I had to make sure my daughter's needs were met while still working toward my own goals. I didn't see this as a challenge but rather an opportunity to grow. I knew I had to maximize every available resource, from scheduling my shifts around my classes to leaning on my parents to help with childcare in the evenings. By being intentional with my studies and leveraging my experience as a young mother, I developed a unique perspective that would prove invaluable in my future career.

As a first-generation graduate, my determination to succeed was fueled by my desire to break the cycle of limited opportunities. However, the transition from college graduate to my professional career was daunting. I wondered, "What now?" and "What's next?" Following my studies in criminology, I explored professional options that seemed impossible to meet with a small child. I felt defeated but not ready to give up. I learned that my degree showed dedication and commitment as an individual. I worked as a customer service representative in a healthcare company but did not see where that would take me. I sent my resumé to my current employer and was offered a position on the sales team.

Starting from this entry-level position, I recognized the value of each opportunity and approached my work with unwavering determination. I was surrounded by successful sales professionals whom I admired. In many ways, the early opportunities were those that came in the form of extra work outside of my normal responsibilities. It energized me to stretch beyond the standard duties and build my knowledge with the goal of furthering my own career. I continued this same mindset with each new opportunity moving forward. I remained curious and open to learning and growing. And I still do.

As I reflect on my experience, I remember how intentionality manifested in various ways. I sought out mentors and sponsors who became a network of guidance and support. I recognized the importance of learning from those who achieved success, though I will admit that I may not have fully understood the power of those networks at the time. The ability to connect with everyone I worked for, with, or alongside allowed me to actively pursue professional development opportunities, attend workshops and conferences, and take on extra responsibilities to expand my knowledge and skill set. There were opportunities to interact with senior leadership, and I realized that if I remained a wallflower and quiet, I wouldn't be recognized. I saw the value in pushing beyond my limits and comforts. Through my continuous learning and growth, I have been able to demonstrate my value within my organization.

As I grow, I continue to consistently set goals and develop action plans to achieve them. My intentionality extends beyond my own success; I seek ways to make a positive impact on my team and broader organization. By fostering strong relationships, displaying exemplary leadership qualities, and embracing challenges as growth opportunities, I gained the respect and recognition of my peers and senior leadership.

Today, my passion has shifted beyond my own personal growth. I firmly believe that my success lies not only in personal achievements but also in recognizing and supporting the success of my team and those around me. While continuing to stretch, I now look for ways and opportunities to advocate for those in situations like mine. I am committed to giving back to communities that are underserved and underprivileged. I understand that, with the right resources and support, individuals in these communities can thrive and achieve remarkable success. By actively participating in initiatives that address their needs and empower them, I will make a lasting impact.

My journey from a lower socioeconomic background to an executive leadership position is a testament to the power of intentionality. I overcame numerous obstacles by making conscious choices and maintaining a steadfast focus on my goals. Beyond my own success, I am so proud of my daughter for studying at the University of Colorado–Boulder with the intention of pursuing her PhD. My family's commitment to academic success continues in her. My hope is that my story illustrates success that is not solely determined by external circumstances but by the intentional actions and decisions we make. It is through determination, resilience, and commitment to personal and professional growth that individuals will overcome obstacles and create their own paths to success. By sharing my story and highlighting the importance of being intentional, I hope to inspire others to believe in themselves, regardless of their starting point.

Jessica Lopez-Liggett is a results-driven executive leader with twenty years of experience in the healthcare industry. She was recently named Indiana Regional Vice President of Sales at Anthem Blue Cross and Blue Shield, where she is responsible for overseeing sales initiatives designed to deliver better health outcomes and affordability for those we serve.

Jessica is a graduate of the University of Missouri–St. Louis and is passionate about serving under-resourced communities. Jessica recently received certification for the McKinsey Hispanic & Latino Executive Leadership Program, which cultivates her excitement for developing future leaders with a focus on diversity and inclusion.

In her personal life, Jessica enjoys traveling, hiking, health and fitness activities, and spending time with her family. Her dedication to her work and her community makes her an invaluable asset to any organization she serves.

Melanie Siebert

Create Your Own Destiny

I laid three large towels down to cover the shower drain, hoping it would give me a few inches of water to bathe my little boy. I was ashamed every time I had to do that. I thought, "What kind of mother am I that we are living like this?" One month before, I'd been evicted from my apartment because my roommate left without a word and stopped paying her portion of the rent. I could see it in my landlord's eyes that they didn't want to make me leave, but they had no other choice as we were already three months' behind. So, there I was, living in a studio apartment in the basement of an old woman's house, bathing my child in the bottom of a shower. How did I get there?

Ever since I was a little girl, I told my family that I was going to be a girl boss, a businesswoman. My mother was a teacher, and my father worked in a hospital. I was grateful for everything I had, but we didn't grow up with a lot. My sister wanted to be a stay-at-home mom with lots of kids, which became reality, and she was perfect at it! That wasn't me, though. My intention was always to get out of a small town and make something of myself, and yet here I was, bathing my little boy on the floor of a shower, feeling like all my dreams were going down the drain.

I was a single mom, working full time as a waitress and bartender, doing everything I could to pay the bill and put groceries on the table.

I was also a full-time student at Kansas State University, trying to finish my bachelor's degree without pulling out my hair or quitting first. Once, a professor told me to quit, as I ran into class a few minutes late. She said I had too much to handle as a single mom and that I should take some time off and "not bite off more than I could chew." At that moment, I felt relieved. She was giving me the green light to stop killing myself to meet this goal of graduating, working, and being a single mom. But later, I was filled with anger. I was so focused on all the challenges that I almost lost sight of the goal: a better life for me and my son and making my dreams of success a reality. It was my choice to be a single mom, and I refused to be a statistic. I would not drive home to small-town Kansas and live with my mother with my head hung low, as if I had no other choice. I had a choice, and that choice was to be a badass who could do it all and look back and say, "We did it!" I realized all the possibilities in front of me, so I set my intention: to power through and get to the other side!

All my managers knew I was in a "work to live" situation, so every time they had an open shift, they called me, and I took it. Sometimes on my way to class I'd get a call for a lunch shift, so I'd quickly change directions to run home, get changed, and be there before the shift started. Though I had no family near me for hundreds of miles in all directions, I had a team of people who rallied around me. In addition to my work family, there was a young man who was in most of my classes that particular semester who had perfect attendance. He asked me why I had missed a few classes, and I told him I needed to work. He offered to take notes for me at the classes I missed. I would collect his notes before a big exam, rewrite them in my notebook, and study all day and night. He did this several times for me, and I will never forget his kindness, nor the look on his face the first time I got a better grade on a test than he did. His eyes grew wide with a dumbfounded expression, mixed with a half smirk. He helped me this way all through my last year of college.

I couldn't always rely on someone else to do the listening for me, so those classes were a little trickier, which meant more night shifts. I couldn't always afford a babysitter, so, again, my league of amazing humans would somehow appear, and someone would roll toy trucks around on the floor with my kiddo while I worked. In those moments, those individuals didn't and will never understand what that support meant to me.

This cycle of work, school, and "momming" went on for a year and a half. Just before graduation, I walked into a meeting with my advisor, so full of excitement that this nightmare was almost over, I was holding in tears. Being a single parent and not always knowing your fate is terrifying. Every decision you make affects this little being who you brought into the world, and there are no do-overs. This reality brought me to my knees many times. To look forward and know that all of that is almost in your rearview mirror and you can finally breathe is an indescribable feeling.

I received my bachelor's degree in Journalism and Mass Communications from Kansas State University in May of 2014. I did not go to my graduation ceremony and throw my hat in the air; I instead went to dinner with family to celebrate the end of one life and the beginning of another. I had overcome all the pessimists and naysayers who said I couldn't do it. I'd realized my dream and lived my intention to be a badass, who did it!

A few years later, I found a career in media marketing that lit a fire in my soul, something I was and am truly passionate about and love doing every day. In 2016, I purchased my first home on my own and was immensely proud to move each and every box into those four walls. I did that. I now work for one of the nation's largest media companies and am proud to say I am a lady boss and have made my own dreams of being successful come true. Today my son has more than he will ever need and will never remember the memories of the cold shower tile in that basement apartment doubling as a makeshift bathtub. He goes to a great school in a Kansas City suburb and has no worries beyond playing with his friends and working on his baseball swing. I know I did that, and I did that for him.

We all have hurdles and challenges in our life, big and small. The way we choose to handle those challenges makes us the people we are. The difficulties we go through shape us and can make us stronger. So here is my advice:

Live with intention! Set your sights on what you want and don't look away until you are holding it in your hand. Imagine what you want and how you will get there. Make a list. I love lists!

Do not make excuses! I know how easy it can be to do that, but you make your own destiny. If you aren't making the time, if you aren't paving your way, no one else will.

Take one day at a time. If you think about the whole picture, you will surely become overwhelmed. Set short-term goals that are achievable with your long-term goals in mind.

Don't get in your own way. For example, if you are constantly breaking your budget for things you want and don't need, or loading your time up with people and events that are moving you in the wrong direction, you are not doing yourself any favors. Every choice you make matters.

Have confidence in yourself. Believing that what you want is possible is a huge part of making it a reality. You *can* get that job. You *do* have what it takes. You *will* study all night to kick butt at fill-in-your-own blank. You are your biggest advocate! Put the time in and you got it!

Surround yourself with positive people and situations. This is a huge one for me. It would have been so much harder to succeed and reach my goals if I did not have my support system. Find those people; they are there. Keep yourself out of situations and away from people that get you off track.

Be direct. Be scrappy. Stay up all night working, or practicing, or planning, or whatever you need to do!

Be proud and grateful when you have arrived at your destination. You did it!

With intention, drive, and grit, you can do anything.

Melanie Siebert is Senior Account Executive and Media Consultant at Audacy, Kansas City. A media advertising and marketing executive for almost ten years, she works with some of the largest businesses in Kansas City as well as the region's professional sports teams. Her favorite part of her job is creating relationships with new clients and individuals and watching them succeed. She loves supporting charities and community events. Melanie and her husband, Roric, live in Shawnee, Kansas, with their three boys and two dogs. Every day is an adventure, filled with work events and supporting her kids in their many extracurricular activities.

Melanie holds a bachelor's degree in Advertising and Marketing from Kansas State University. She volunteers for several Shawnee committees and organizations and is a huge advocate and supporter of animal adoption, working closely with several rescues in the Kansas City metro area.

Vidya Thandra Satyanarayana

Rise and Shine

Just five years ago, I was a mom struggling to land a job after a decade-long break from the workforce. It was never easy, but now that I look at my struggles, it was all worth it. As a stay-at-home mom turned IT professional who manages teams across the world, I am here to share my story to let fellow moms and aspiring women know that if I can do it, you can do it too.

"It's a challenge to get back to the workforce if you had a break in your career." Have you heard this phrase before? If you nodded "yes" and think that's true, let me tell you, it's not. With the right attitude and the right tools, nothing is impossible. When I decided to get back into the workforce, I wanted to carve my path to success and create an identity for myself. The intention I set for myself became clear: to be financially independent to support myself, help others when possible, and experience joy through the process.

As I started my journey back into the workforce, I explored all my options. My background was not in Information Technology (IT), and I wanted to get into IT. That's a big challenge on its own. Now combine it with a decade break, new country, unfamiliar faces, and my introvert personality, and the challenge becomes even more complex. Instead of freaking out, I kept my focus on my intention and reminded myself to take things one step at a time.

First step: I spoke with my family and friends—people who knew me well. The more conversations I had, the more clarity I got on what I should do. Based on the data collected from all my interactions, I registered for online courses to help me understand the various roles I could pursue. I finished many projects around the clock, working with the constructive feedback I got from the teachers. I loved it. It helped me understand the areas I was lacking and how to improve. As I said, the process was not easy, but it was so worth it.

As a mom with a little kid, there were days when I would work on my projects after he went to bed. I hoped to get feedback back from the project reviewer before my toddler woke up so I could work on the feedback. I remember when I passed a specific project and earned the nanodegree certificate. I got the email at around two a.m. and wanted to scream and celebrate, but my son was sleeping in the next room! I celebrated very calmly, and it was such a happy time for me to accomplish something I worked so hard for. It was the fruit of all my hard work and persistence despite the many challenges and hurdles I faced.

There were times I gave up. That's the truth. But I would restart again in a day or two after remembering my intention and why I started this process in the first place. I didn't want to give up after going so far in my journey. Also, I had a pair of little cute eyes watching what mommy was doing. I wanted to inspire him through the process too.

In the quest to solve this puzzle of breaking through the job market after a decade break and trying to update my professional knowledge, I also reached out to a local nonprofit aimed at helping women get back into the workforce. This organization trained and certified me in data analysis. Among my classmates were women who had similar stories to mine and who shared my intention. Women supporting women was magic. This certification process also provided an opportunity to interact with instructors who were working on projects that involved all those technologies. I knew I was in the right place. Getting certified and standing with my certificate, surrounded by people from diverse backgrounds clapping and cheering for me, is one of the proudest moments of my life. Even better, I invited my parents to join me and participate in my joyful moment of this major achievement eight thousand miles from where I was born.

The other big challenge I faced was speaking in front of people. Before I landed a job, I wanted to improve in this area. I decided to address this in combination with what I loved doing best—volunteering at a local butterfly house. Butterflies have always given me a very positive, beautiful vibe and calmed me down. Also, I believe butterflies are our ancestors who are staying close to us. I began speaking about the various insects to the visitors at the Butterfly House. One fine day, they handed me a beetle and asked me to talk about it to the visitors. I hate beetles! But that was the whole point of me volunteering—to face my fears. My intention was very clear. After some self-talk, I called on my courage and perseverance. Speaking to the visitors, I successfully handled Death Feining Beetles, safely let visitors handle them, talked about their habitats, and returned them back to their cages. As someone who would run away if I saw a beetle in my house, I smiled and patted myself on the back. Because of my success, I was invited to join the team to work on documents for the various insects and butterflies for publication on their website. Halfway through my time volunteering at the Butterfly House, I got an opportunity to be interviewed for a financial company. In a few weeks, I got the offer and was asked for references. My manager at the Butterfly House was the first one to give me a great reference. The beetles were so worth it.

That's how my journey began. With every new challenge, I saw an opportunity to find a solution. This helped me keep going. Through the process, I also learned the importance of being mentored. There were mentors all along my journey who were telling me there is light at the end of the tunnel and kept guiding me toward it. That meant the world to me.

Today, I am an IT Professional managing teams across the world. It brings me joy to do this every day. It's been a challenging journey, but I am grateful for every experience, every opportunity, and every person who helped me along the way. My clear intention helped me through some dark days.

I overcame the taboo of doubts about women reentering the workforce after taking a break. I want to shine my light on others who are hesitant to take their first steps into a new career. I am happy to hold their hand, tell them to take a deep breath, and smile as we take steps together and prove that "It's OK. We got this."

To anyone out there who is thinking of returning to work after a break, my advice is to believe in yourself, stay focused on your intention, and be willing to put in the work. Don't be afraid to ask for help or guidance. It's never too late to pursue your dreams. Returning to work after a long break can be challenging; it was for me. You can be successful. Be patient, take the next steps, and don't give up on your goal of achieving financial independence and personal fulfillment.

Through my process of chasing my dream, I want to give credit to three very important people in my life. First and foremost, my parents. No matter their challenges or how bad their day was, my mom and dad supported me to the fullest. My slightest doubts vanished when I shared my day with them and saw a proud smile on their faces. They are my biggest blessing.

The next big support came from my husband, who kept assuring me that he had my back, dropped me off for my classes after his work, and waited outside till I was done to bring me home safely. He wiped my tears away many times and gave me his shoulder to rest my head on.

Last but most important is my son. After a long day of work or struggle, I always looked forward to coming home and his big, tight bear hug. His hugs gave me the energy to fight for my dreams again the next day. At the playground, he inspired me to take chances when he climbed the monkey bar or slid down the tallest slide without hesitation. He taught me more about life and to enjoy the little things that we take for granted.

Summing up my words, I have just one quote to share which has always inspired me:

"Arise, Awake and Stop not till the goal is reached."

—*Swami Vivekananda*

Good luck to all those who are facing challenges, big or small. Know that I am always cheering for you.

If I can do it, you can do it too.

Vidya is a mom who returned to the workforce after a decade-long break. She holds a bachelor's degree in Business and is also a Certified Chartered Accountant from India. After moving to the United States, raising a family, and defeating all social taboos for women returning to the workforce after a break, she is now a successful IT professional.

Vidya has been featured in Forbes and other media channels, sharing her journey to empower women. She believes in paying it forward and speaks to groups across the globe on encouraging women and helping them see their power rise.

Vidya is a trained Indian classical music singer and loves to experiment in mixed media art. Her recent passion includes cooking, photography, and learning new technologies.

Maura Caldwell-Thompson

Letting Go of Holding On

Intention: to aim or plan. Many people think of intention as something to grip onto and fight for, something you don't let go of. But my story is about finding balance between having a goal and being able to let it go. My story is about being able to change and adapt while not holding on too tightly. When I first thought about writing this chapter, I pictured myself in a quiet corner writing under soft lighting, inspired after a quiet day of reflection. The reality is I am huddled in a corner of a high school cafeteria during my oldest child's dance competition. Inspiration strikes where it will. Watching these young children strive for the goal of making it in the dance world, of being recognized for their craft, I am inspired to share my story. I want them to know what I learned and not have to suffer in the same ways. And yet I know in my heart we all must find our own way.

When teaching yoga classes, I talk about finding your edge. In yoga, finding your edge means pushing your body, perhaps challenging your flexibility or strength, but not too far. You want to challenge yourself but not pull a muscle at the same time. So how do we find that place? How do we find our edge in life?

I have debated this question for hours with many people. As a therapist who specializes in eating disorders, my clients have been some of the smartest, most ambitious, and talented people. And yet that very drive toward their goals is what brings them to my office for treatment. They need to realign, to readjust—to set a new intention. As a former professional dancer turned yoga teacher, therapist, and queer-identifying mom of five, I, too, have had to adjust, to reconfigure, to reset, to burn it all down and start again. Being able to reflect and set a new intention for the day is what makes it all worthwhile.

I find the phoenix, the bird in Greek mythology that is immortal yet has a cycle of regeneration or rebirth, to be beautiful, intriguing, and admirable. Yet there was a time in my life when I was terrified of the very concept. As the oldest of four children in an upper middle class suburban Catholic family, I was great at following the rules. When I played soccer, I refused to move because "the coach told me to stand right here." That's why ballet appealed to me. It was—or rather I thought it was—black and white, right or wrong, and the dancer was constantly striving for perfection. I spent so many hours of my childhood studying, striving, learning, and perfecting the art of ballet. In elementary school, I set my alarm a half hour earlier so I would have time to stretch before school. In middle school, I said no to plans with friends to dedicate my time to classes and performances. In high school, I learned that to make it in the dance world I needed to work harder and push more, all while eating as little as possible.

As my star grew brighter and I got noticed for my talents and skills in dance, my body got smaller and smaller. I was wrapped up in anorexia, thinking it was making me a better dancer, until it wasn't. In my senior year of high school, I was accepted into a prestigious college dance program. I passionately continued crafting my art, struggling to get the "shapes" right, always thinking if I were just smaller, I could float higher. I worked hard, went on to dance with a company, and was elated! Then one day it all came crashing down. One moment I was in the studio rehearsing, and the next someone was taking my pointe shoes off and I was in an ambulance headed to the nearest hospital. The doctors informed me that my eating disorder had gotten so extreme that my body was eating my heart muscle to stay alive. In one moment, the career I had been working and preparing for since childhood, that I thought was my path in life, was over. I had no sense of identity outside of dance. I felt like I had no purpose in life at all.

I spent the next few years in and out of treatment centers, hospitals, and therapy. Recovery was not an easy journey. But in this process, I found yoga. In yoga I was able to work on healing my relationship with my body in a way that made sense. It wasn't dance, but it used the body awareness I had from years of training in ballet to help me reconnect, find self-compassion, forgive myself, find gratitude for my body and myself, and experience wonder and awe. Yoga opened new doors for me. I decided to become a yoga teacher to share this incredible gift with others. At this time, I also decided to pursue my psychology degree. I had a new path, I had a purpose, I was ready.

I graduated college, got married, and we moved to a new city where I started my doctoral program. I had a plan; I had intention. I was back on track and "following the rules." Then, unexpectedly, and somewhat miraculously, I got pregnant. New plot twist! I decided I could not live in a new city, with no family nearby, with a new baby while still pursuing my doctorate. So we moved back home. I pursued my master's degree to become licensed and work in the mental health field while I had young kids. I graduated when my daughter was two and started my private practice right away. I was better at adapting this time. It wasn't that I knew what to expect, but I did know that I could change course and that did not mean I had failed. I had my daughter to think of; I wasn't just doing this for myself anymore.

The next few years went smoothly. We bought a house. I had two more children. My private practice thrived, and it gave me the flexibility to work and to be with my kids. I reconnected with dance by teaching while continuing to teach yoga. I was right on track, but something was missing. I looked at my then-seven-year-old daughter, the one I told every day to follow her heart, her dreams, her passions, and to live her authentic life to find true happiness, and realized I wasn't doing that very thing. How could I encourage her to follow her truth and be brave if I wasn't doing that myself?

I realized what was missing in my marriage, and I knew I had to be honest. So I took the very difficult step of coming out at the age of thirty-two. I came out to my then-husband and got divorced. I came out to my very Catholic family. I came out to my friends and people who had known me my whole life as "the good girl" and "the rule follower." This time, I broke all the rules. I felt a little like a black sheep, but also free and alive in a way I had never known. We went through some rough moments on this leg of the journey, and I certainly worried if I had "let go" too much. Little by little, things came together. I met my now-wife, and together we created the life I never knew I needed. The clouds parted, and for the first time in my entire life I felt truly happy and whole. We got married and blended our families into a very chaotic, very loving group of people we affectionately call "The Wildwood 7."

I still have my private practice, but I am also an adjunct professor in a dance department where I teach students about somatics—a concept of using mind-body connection for healing and awareness. I also serve as a mental health liaison providing education for students in the department around anxiety, depression, eating disorders, and stress management strategies.

Things have truly come full circle. At twenty-one, when I was being whisked away from the dance studio, I could have never dreamed my career, my family, or my loving partner into being. Now, when I sit with clients in their twenties who are struggling with their identity or what to do with their life, or when I talk with other moms who feel lost with what to do next as their kids prepare to leave for college, I am often asked, "How did you know what you wanted to do with your life? How did you find your joy?" The truth is: I let go. I let go of the idea that I could control things into being the way I wanted. I focused on my values, I set my intention, and then I let myself live.

Maura Caldwell-Thompson is an adjunct professor in the Department of Dance at Webster University. A St. Louis native, Maura has taught dance in the area for more than twenty years to all levels and ages. Maura also has professional dance experience with MADCO. In addition to her dance career, Maura holds a master's degree in clinical counseling and is the owner of Balance Within, LLC where she specializes in the treatment of eating disorders, trauma, grief, anxiety, and depression. Through Washington University, she also provides therapy services for families of children receiving care in St. Louis Children's Hospital Heart Center. Maura is an arts and education advocate with a passion for promoting health and wellness within dance and performance. She lives in St. Louis with her wife and their five kids.

Gina Sweet

Intentional Love

I'll be honest: I haven't always lived with intention. Looking back, I'd say I was just flapping in the winds and seas of life and getting caught in many storms. I lived for approval and validation, in an unhealthy state of comparison and people pleasing. When it came to intention, my good ones disappeared into thin air like a dandelion poof. This kind of living left me wanting more out of life and reminded me of all I lacked. I had a hard time distinguishing truth in my life and bought in to lies that bound me to a mental prison of hopelessness. I didn't know it, but I had unintentionally surrendered my right to truly love myself and love my life. This was me before I encountered Jesus Christ.

Now I see intention as a passionate pursuit that seeks truth and follows purpose-filled steps to reach a desired outcome.

"Jesus told him, 'I am the WAY, the TRUTH, and the LIFE. No one can come to the Father except through me.'" John 14:6 (NLT)

People can feel uncomfortable talking about Jesus, but in a culture where we praise just about anything and anyone who does whatever they want, I'd like to give my Jesus a shout-out! There is no one in this world who lived a more intentional life than him. Jesus teaches us that intentional faith should be deeply rooted with eternity in mind. Someday, we will all stand before our creator, whether we believe in him or not. We will all be judged, our intentions exposed, and we will give an accounting to God for what we put our faith in here on Earth.

"For this is how God loved the world: He gave his one and only Son, so that everyone who believes in him will not perish but have eternal life." John 3:16 (NLT)

I never in a million years imagined that faith would be the most intentional part of my life, but it is. My faith is not a religion or a building; it's a relationship with my creator. My story is one of amazing healing through intentional faith in Jesus.

I was born in Bogota, Colombia. My parents and I moved to Miami, Florida, when I was four. Beginning as a toddler, I was exposed to both physical and verbal abuse. My father was an alcoholic, and my mother, a shell of a human being, endured the abuse and also dished it out. When I was nine, my father stopped by my grade school while I was in PE to say goodbye forever. I felt so unwanted and unloved. My mother had taught me that "dirty laundry is washed at home," so I kept every emotion bottled up so that no one would see. I was always guarded, especially with my mother. Let's just say she wasn't the softest pillow to land on.

I didn't know how damaging all these unspoken feelings were to me as I was going through life, because that was just life. I had no clue that kids lived in happy, abuse-free homes where they could share their feelings and where their parents nurtured them. As a parent myself, I now see what a healthy home should be. It has been quite a journey to forgive my parents and myself.

My life was filled with resentment, anger, shame, guilt, and a bitterness that blinded me. It stirred in me an unhealthy desire for approval, validation, and control. I was being manipulated and neglected by my mother; I saw obedience and submission as the ways to earn my mother's love. I didn't see the sexual abuse; I saw approval. I didn't see the physical abuse;

I saw what I thought I deserved. I didn't see myself; I saw shame and disgust, which led to years of bulimia and eating disorders. I fell for everything and lost so much of myself. I had an abortion because my mother threatened to disown me if I kept my baby. How I regret that decision.

I believed love was something that had to be earned, and by perfect obedience, goodness, beauty, and strength. I felt unworthy of this kind of love and began to consider suicide when I was thirteen, after my dad died. I went into weeks of depression thinking about life after death. After the abortion, my suicidal ideations increased and I couldn't look in the mirror without hating the person staring back at me.

"He [the devil] was a murderer from the beginning. He has always hated the truth, because there is no truth in him. When he lies, it is consistent with his character; for he is a liar and the father of lies." John 8:44 (NLT)

My eyes were opened to truth when my husband had his first heart attack at the age of twenty-seven, and then another at twenty-nine due to a hereditary disease. I hit rock bottom. I cried out to God, literally on my knees at the hospital the day of Jason's heart attack. "God, if you are real, please help me!" I hadn't grown up in church. I knew about religion but wasn't religious or spiritual.

Even as I prayed, I wondered how a Heavenly Father could love me, let alone hear me or care about my problems if my own earthly father hadn't. I felt so alone and afraid. In my twisted thinking, I thought if God is love, and love is conditional, then surely I am unworthy of it.

It's been almost sixteen years since I first cried out to God from the depths of my soul. I did it selfishly, in anguish and in doubt. But I did it anyway, and he showed up and hasn't left my side. He didn't just save my husband from dying from a heart attack once, but twice. He released me from my shame, my guilt, and my resentment and gave me a heart of forgiveness and love. He freed me from my need to prove my worth and showed me that I am worth dying for as shown by Jesus's death on the cross. Friend, our greatest accomplishments and victories cannot heal our deepest hurts and struggles. Only God can. Without healing in our hearts, our victories are a counterfeit shadow of success compared to the victories we have when we are healed and whole.

This is why no matter how high we get up the ladder of success, we can still feel empty. We might have a loving family and a beautiful home and still want more, or have a full bank account and still feel as if it's not enough. Our greatest desire is to be well known and well loved. By pursuing the truth found in Jesus's perfect love, we can fully embrace our lives with deep gratitude. We mustn't pridefully hide our life's suffering as a badge of honor. We can embrace the one who suffered patiently and understood the outcome of his suffering: the saving of our very souls. His name is Jesus, and through his life and example, I have received a healing that has produced a love for him, myself, my family, and for others that I just can't contain. This is a treasure that I must share because the freedom it produces transcends time and opens the door to eternity here on Earth.

I have been born again into a perfect love. The lies that blinded me have been replaced with truth that guides, protects, strengthens, and sets me free daily.

"And you will know the truth, and the truth will set you free". John 8:32 (NLT)

My friend, if you are tired of carrying that baggage, are ready to be set free, want to give some purpose to your pain, and are open to a relationship with Jesus, here are some ways you might turn to him:

- Invite him into your life. Be REAL, be vulnerable. Be grateful!
- Buy a bible and *read* it. Don't be afraid to write in the margins the thoughts that come to mind. The Holy Spirit is alive and active and helps us understand the bible.

- Dedicate time to study the bible. Currently, I like to give myself an hour before my home wakes up to spend time in the Word.

- Pray. Praying isn't a repetitive series of words to get what you want; it is constant communication with God.

"Always be joyful. Never stop praying. Be thankful in all circumstances, for this is God's will for you who belong to Christ Jesus." 1 Thessalonians 5:16–18 (NLT)

- Fast. Learn about biblical fasting. We are spirit beings and must take in spiritual food.

- "Jesus replied, 'I am the bread of life. Whoever comes to me will never be hungry again. Whoever believes in me will never be thirsty.'" John 6:35 (NLT)

If you walk around spiritually starved, you will feast on what the world serves you, which never satisfies. Fasting requires a surrender to our need for food or pleasure. It is not only about what you give up but about what you give yourself to.

"People do not live by bread alone, but by every word that comes from the mouth of God." Matthew 4:4 (NLT)

My friend, if you've been hurt by religion, or a person of faith, I am truly sorry. I'm sorry if you were unheard, confused, lied to, abused, or taken advantage of. Please don't let this keep you from a relationship with your creator. The person or institution that hurt you are not God. He is faithful to complete every good work he starts and will redeem what has hurt you if you turn to him. He is a gentleman and loves you enough to let you choose. May our Heavenly Father bless you and guide you as you take this message and respond to it. No one has better intentions for you than your Heavenly Father. Don't take my word for it. Ask him and he *will* show you.

Gina Sweet thanks God for the GRIT he has given her and for giving her contentment and gratitude in everything she's done so far in this life. Gina served our country as a soldier in the US Army. She is a registered nurse and a recipient of the Daisy Award for her compassion and dedication to her patients. She is a mentor and leader within the body of Christ and has served in various roles to include children's, women's, and youth ministries. Adding author to this list, she confesses, is a dream come true and just the beginning of what's to come.

Gina says, "I have had many roles in life but none that I love more than being a wife and mom."

Married for twenty years to her soulmate, Jason, they have been entrusted with five treasures in their children: Kevin, Lincoln, Julie, Jordan, and Lia.

Gina's heart's intention is for all people to be-LOVE-d. A play on words for what it truly means to intentionally love others as we have been loved.

Join the movement and share how God transforms your life when you intentionally surrender to him.

All for his Glory!

TEAM OF SEVEN

Rachel Rubin Wilkins

Freelance Consultant

We believe that a team with an innovative marketing
strategy can make an impact on the world.

TEAMOFSEVEN.COM – TEAMOFSEVEN.GOALS@GMAIL.COM

"Strength and honor are her clothing.
She is confident about the future."

Proverbs 31:25

Taryn Pulliam

A Path Of My Own

INTENTION

GADELLNET

Made in the USA
Monee, IL
06 September 2023